Teaching Critical Thinking:

Using Seminars for 21st Century Literacy

Terry Roberts and Laura Billings

GOVERNORS STATE UNIVERSITY
UNIVERSITY PARK, IL

EYE ON EDUCATION
6 DEPOT WAY WEST, SUITE 106
LARCHMONT, NY 10538
(914) 833–0551
(914) 833–0761 fax
www.eyeoneducation.com

Sponsoring Editor: Robert Sickles
Production Editor: Lauren Davis
Copyeditor: Sarah Wolbach
Compositor: Richard Adin, Freelance Editorial Services
Cover Designer: Armen Kojoyian

Library of Congress Cataloging-in-Publication Data

Roberts, Terry, 1956-
   Teaching critical thinking : using seminars for 21st century literacy / Terry Roberts and Laura Billings.
      p. cm.
   Includes bibliographical references.
   ISBN 978-1-59667-208-6
   1. Critical thinking—Study and teaching. 2. Language arts. 3. Seminars.
I. Billings, Laura. II. Title.
   LB1590.3.R635 2012
   370.15′2—dc23

                                                    2011037761

10 9 8 7 6 5 4 3 2 1

Also Available from EYE ON EDUCATION

Active Literacy Across the Curriculum:
Strategies for Reading, Writing, Speaking, and Listening
Heidi Hayes Jacobs

But I'm Not a Reading Teacher:
Strategies for Literacy Instruction in the Content Areas
Amy Benjamin

Literacy from A to Z
Barbara R. Blackburn

Family Reading Night
Darcy Hutchins, Marsha Greenfeld, and Joyce Epstein

Rigor is NOT a Four-Letter Word
Barbara R. Blackburn

Writing in the Content Areas, Second Edition
Amy Benjamin

Literacy Leadership Teams:
Collaborative Leadership for Improving and
Sustaining Student Achievement
Pamela S. Craig

Vocabulary at the Center
Amy Benjamin, John T. Crow

Writer's Workshop for the Common Core:
A Step-by-Step Guide
Warren E. Combs

Awakening Brilliance in the Writer's Workshop:
ng Notebooks, Mentor Texts, and the Writing Process
Lisa Morris

"We should examine more thoroughly what are the natural principles of human fellowship and community. First is something that is seen in the fellowship of the entire human race. For its bonding consists of reason and speech, which reconcile men to one another, through teaching, learning, communicating, debating and making judgments, and unite them in a kind of natural fellowship. It is this that most distances us from the nature of other animals."

—Cicero, *De Officiis*

About the Authors

Dr. Terry Roberts has been Director of the National Paideia Center since 1993. A former high school English teacher from Asheville, North Carolina, he is a practicing scholar of American Literature and Cultural Studies, with a strong penchant for the classics. He is fascinated by the social and intellectual power of dialogue to teach and to inspire.

Dr. Laura Billings has been Associate Director of the National Paideia Center since 1998. She is a former secondary teacher from Jacksonville, Florida. Dr. Billings' research and teaching focus on the socio-linguistic aspects of dialogue. In addition, she is deeply committed to holistic assessment practices.

Together, they are the authors of numerous books and articles about dialogue and literacy.

Free Download and Video

The Seminar Process Assessment form discussed and displayed on page 67 of this book is also available on Eye On Education's website as an Adobe Acrobat file. Permission has been granted to purchasers of this book to download this resource and print it.

You can access this download by visiting Eye On Education's website: www.eyeoneducation.com. From the home page, click on Free, and then choose Supplemental Downloads. Alternatively, you can search or browse our website to find this book, and then scroll for downloading instructions. You'll need your book buyer access code: TCT-7208-6.

To watch a video of a Paideia Seminar in action, go to www.paideia.org and click on For Teachers.

Contents

Introduction

The Role of Thinking in Today's Schools

You hold in your hands a book intended for those who are interested in the practice of critical thinking skills through dialogue. Most of our examples come from the classroom and so will interest teachers first and foremost, but we also offer examples of adult discussions that are just as purposeful and intellectually fervent as those involving younger students.

We are concerned in these pages with the ability of the individual human being to think, both alone and in concert with others, and how that ability can be nurtured over time. We have written this book because we believe that it is possible to teach the vast majority of children and adolescents in our schools to think more clearly and coherently about sophisticated issues. We also believe that it is possible for us to continue honing our ability to think, extending the initial process of schooling into the deeper learning of adulthood.

Our goal in writing this book is to help teachers prepare their students to lead richer, more thoughtful lives in at least three ways:

- by being good citizens when democratic citizenship—whether local or global—requires objectivity and understanding

- by leading good lives, honoring our own hearts, minds, and souls as well as those of others

- by earning decent livings in what many commentators are calling the "Cognitive Age"

Indeed, the enhancement of citizenship, quality of life, and livelihood should be the goal of all *true* education, which is to say, lifelong education.[1]

---

1 As originally inspired by *The Paideia Proposal* (1982)

Learning to think, however, takes consistent practice, and growth in the ability to think is usually a long journey rather than a quick fix. Learning to think involves practicing a range of skills, especially speaking and listening, eventually at very sophisticated levels. We believe we can practice thinking skills productively, in part because we already know a lot about the speaking and listening skills that make up the thinking process. When these skills are practiced together, the result—an enhanced ability to think—is much greater than the sum of its parts.

The primary place that teaching and learning to think come into play is our schools. Here, habits of mind are first formed in a deliberate way. There are, unfortunately, objections to teaching critical thinking in our schools. Among the most prevalent are the following: that teaching critical thinking is too time consuming; that thinking skills are too difficult to measure; and that not all students are capable of learning to think conceptually. None of these concerns are legitimate, and in fact, when we examine them closely, they lead us back to our original thesis: Not only is it possible to teach thinking; it is also the wisest course available to us.

The first question is whether we have time in school to learn to think. On the cusp of the 21st century, when everything we project about the human experience, both public and private, suggests the need for speed, can we afford quite literally to slow down and invest in teaching and learning thinking, a process that can be slow and even laborious? The answer is that we can't afford not to—now more than ever.

Everything we know about life in the 21st century tells us that our students must be prepared with a wide range of communication and thinking skills if they are to have a chance in the workplace and if they are to contribute to a functioning democracy. What we are going to describe in this book is, in many ways, a classical education intended for the 21st century world. It involves returning to ancient wisdom as a response to contemporary challenges.

21st Century Skills

The Partnership for 21st Century Skills—a coalition of American businesses with an international focus, funded in part by the U.S. Department of Education—has been at work articulating the skills that will be most in demand during the new century.[2] In *21st Century Skills, Education & Competitiveness: a Resource and Policy Guide*, the Partnership states bluntly that "the nation needs to do a much better job teaching and measuring advanced 21st century skills that are the indispensible currency for participation, achieve-

---

2 For a full discussion of these skills and the growing movement to implement a new and different kind of education based upon them, visit the 21st Century Skills website at www.21stcenturyskills.org

ment, and competitiveness in the global economy" and goes on to summarize those skills:

- ◆ **Thinking critically and making judgments** about the barrage of information that comes their way every day—on the Web, in the media, in homes, in workplaces, and everywhere else. Critical thinking empowers Americans to assess the credibility, accuracy, and value of information; to analyze and evaluate information; to make reasoned decisions; and to take purposeful action.

- ◆ **Solving complex, multidisciplinary, open-ended problems** that all workers, in every kind of workplace, routinely encounter. The challenges workers face don't come in a multiple-choice format and typically don't have a single right solution. Nor can they be neatly categorized as "math problems," for example, or passed off to someone at a higher pay grade. Businesses expect employees at all levels to identify problems, think through solutions and alternatives, and explore new options if their approaches don't pan out. Often, this work involves groups of people with different knowledge and skills who, collectively, add value to their organizations.

- ◆ **Employing creativity and entrepreneurial thinking**—a skill set highly associated with job creation. Many of the fastest-growing jobs and emerging industries rely on workers' creative capacity—the ability to think unconventionally, question the herd, imagine new scenarios, and produce astonishing work. Likewise, Americans can create jobs for themselves and others who have an entrepreneurial mindset—for example, the ability to recognize and act on opportunities and the willingness to embrace risk and responsibility.

- ◆ **Making innovative use of knowledge, information, and opportunities** to create new services, processes, and products. The global marketplace rewards organizations that rapidly and routinely find better ways of doing things. Companies want workers who can contribute in this environment.

These skills will withstand the test of time, fluctuations in the economy and the marketplace, and dynamic employment demands.

Most of these skills are couched in the more public world of work, but they clearly play a role in an individual's private life as well. The ability to communicate successfully and think coherently contributes to a man or woman leading a rich personal life as well as a public one.

The Common Core State Standards

For all those reasons, we are especially pleased with the Common Core State Standards (CCSS) that were released in 2010. We believe that the Paideia (puh-day-uh) Seminar is a natural and effective part of any module of study that is designed to deliver the Common Core State Standards because the seminar embodies the reading, speaking, and listening standards that are at the heart of the Common Core. Indeed, any unit of study that doesn't stress speaking and listening as well as reading and writing will, by default, fail to deliver the full range of literacy standards.

> *The seminar embodies the reading, speaking, and listening standards that are at the heart of the Common Core.*

Those skills that will be most in demand in this century—21st Century Basics, we might call them—take time to learn and time to teach. They are deep rather than surface skills, and require an ample time investment on the part of schools and school systems. Ironically, in order to teach our students how to flourish in a "fast" world, we will first have to teach them—and ourselves—how to slow down.

Thinking and Assessments

The second common question about teaching thinking in our schools has to do with assessment: Can we measure a student's ability to think critically and creatively? We believe the answer is yes, in part because we already know a good deal about how to measure skills that make up the thinking process—especially speaking and writing. Reading comprehension and writing ability may be easier (faster and less expensive) to assess because they can be measured through a written test or assignment. Yet, with a little more time and effort, we can apply strong measurement principles to intellectual understanding as it grows through conversation.

Beyond assessing the quality of an individual's thought through the quality of his or her reading, writing, speaking, and listening skills, we believe it is possible to describe successful thinking in a clear, measurable way. All assessment strategies simply require a certain level of commitment, and a willingness to go on learning throughout adulthood; coaching these fundamental literacy skills by example as well as direct instruction. In other words, learning to think is a lifelong endeavor—and a vital one for educators.

Thinking in Children

Even when you accept that it is possible to define, teach, and measure thinking skills, there remains a third question about making the teaching of thinking a consistent part of schooling. This last objection is more insidious than the first two and indeed often goes unspoken. It is based on the common assumption that not all children or adolescents can learn to think at a high level. In other words, this point of view maintains that some children have the innate capacity for higher order thinking skills and some do not, and no amount of instruction or practice can change what is assumed to be a predetermined outcome.

There are three blunt points to be made in response to this assumption. First, the brain research of the last quarter century consistently suggests that our previous beliefs about innate potential were seriously flawed, and that indeed, the vast majority of human beings are capable of abstract and higher-order thought as well as sophisticated expression. What limits the growth of literacy and thinking skills is not capacity but experience—in school and elsewhere. For the second point, we need to refer again to the Partnership for 21st Century Skills and their plea for a universal transformation in how we teach thinking and communication: "All Americans, not just an elite few, need 21st century skills that will increase their marketability, employability and readiness for citizenship."

There is a third, practical point in reply to the mistaken notion that not all children can learn to think. We believe learning to think is much like learning to read or write—in part because these skills are intimately related. In this century, we should no more accept the notion that some of our children won't learn to think clearly and coherently about abstract ideas than we should accept the notion that they won't learn to read. Critical thinking is as fundamental and basic a skill as reading, and like reading, it is a skill that *must* be consistently taught and practiced.

> *Critical thinking is as fundamental and basic a skill as reading, and like reading, it is a skill that must be consistently taught and practiced.*

In "The Paideia Principles" (1988), Mortimer Adler and his colleagues argue eloquently that "schooling at its best is preparation for becoming generally educated in the course of a whole lifetime."[3] Never was this statement more true than in relation to learning to think. Ultimately, the goal of education is wisdom, and that comes from the continued practice—throughout one's life—of the skills we describe here.

What's Inside This Book

In this book, we will explore what actually happens as students are learning to participate in formal seminar discussion—first with proficiency and then with some expertise. We will examine how independent and interdependent thought grow in relation to each other as students become more

3 See pages 309–10 in *Reforming Education: The Opening of the American Mind.*

experienced in seminar practice. After discussing assessment and a detailed description of what might be termed the finished product, we provide appendices of practical materials gleaned from decades of experience, both in schools and elsewhere.

1

What Is Thinking? Can We Teach It in School?

"Intellect presupposes Literacy."
—Jacques Barzun

Perhaps the hardest part of designing a program for teaching thinking is to define simply and clearly what thinking is. Philosophers have been doing that for centuries; our real challenge is to define thinking in a way that helps us understand how someone learns to think more skillfully and how to teach those skills. Attempts to teach thinking are as old as the ancient world and as recent as yesterday; unfortunately, most of the attempts have had little influence on what currently goes on in classrooms.

Our challenge in preparing to write this book has been to create a definition of thinking that most teachers and most students can understand, and then use the definition itself as a tool for improving their own thinking. With this in mind, we have come to define *thinking* as "the ability to explain and manipulate a text." By *text*, we mean "a set of interrelated ideas, often represented in a human artifact." Learning to think, then, is the process of successfully explaining and manipulating increasingly complex texts. By definition, increasingly complex texts contain more discrete elements and more complex relationships between and among those elements. Perhaps this definition makes more sense when you realize what we mean by the word *text*; used here, it is not limited to works in the form of printed language. Obviously, a fable by Aesop, Lincoln's Second Inaugural Address, and the Pythagorean Theorem are all texts. But the Periodic Table of the Elements and a painting by Leonardo da Vinci are also texts. Needless to say, the standardized curriculum is full of texts (books, problems, experiments, and other human artifacts) that represent the core ideas and values that shape the curriculum.

In fact, a text can be almost any human artifact that is rich enough in ideas, complex enough in relationships, and ambiguous enough in meaning to support extended examination and discussion. In history, this designation includes things as varied as maps, treaties, court decisions, and speeches; in science, it includes things as varied as diagrams, charts, classifications, and data tables; in mathematics, it includes things as varied as definitions, formulas, graphs, and problems of all kinds; in literature, it includes things as varied as dictionaries, poems, novels, and plays. Even this list is not exhaustive; rather, it is only suggestive of the rich possibilities that infuse any curriculum or discipline. In order to generate the kind of discussion that both inspires and teaches thinking, a text must be rich in ideas and values, complex in the relationships between those ideas and values, and ambiguous enough to defy easy explanation (see Appendix A for a list of ideas and values for discussion). The point is that just as any curriculum is built on a foundation of ideas, those ideas live in the dozens of texts that must be studied in order to master that curriculum if mastery means true understanding and not mere memorization.

With this distinction in mind, let's return to our original definition of *thinking*: "the ability to explain and manipulate a text." And the definition of *learning to think*: "the process of successfully explaining and manipulating increasingly complex texts."

How Can Students Learn to Think About Texts?

Explaining and manipulating a text often involves the intellectual skills that are commonly referenced in education circles. For this reason, many of the terms that we have traditionally used to discuss thinking in school make perfect sense in the context of this definition. For example, we often ask our students to *describe, clarify, predict, analyze, synthesize,* and so on. If you imagine applying these skills to a text like a Shakespearean sonnet, they immediately take on clarity.

Let's hand our high school English class Shakespeare's Sonnet 130 ("My mistress' eyes are nothing like the sun...") and a definition of an English or Shakespearean sonnet (three quatrains followed by a rhymed couplet). If we break the class into collaborative groups and give each group a thinking process to practice, we should elicit something like the following: One group describes the four sections of the sonnet using the language of the definition. Another group clarifies the rhyme scheme of the poem by labeling the rhymes within each section and chanting the rhymes for the class. Another group reads only the first twelve lines of the poem and predicts what the closing couplet will say. Another group analyzes the diction of the sonnet by creating a T-chart of sensory language used to describe the idealized woman versus the speaker's mistress. Yet another group synthesizes the whole by showing the relationship of the closing couplet to the first three quatrains of the poem with words or graphic images. The point is that all of these thinking processes are ways of explaining the "text" that is the poem. Having thoroughly explained Shakespeare's sonnet, our students might well be ready to write their own, thereby manipulating the sonnet form.

Just as there is a fairly common language that educators use to describe various thinking skills in the classroom, there are also several well-known—and quite valuable—taxonomies of thinking skills that almost any teacher will recognize if not quote on demand. The best known of these, of course, is Bloom's Taxonomy, originally developed in 1956 by a group of educational psychologists headed by Benjamin Bloom. Bloom's original six levels (*knowledge, understanding, application, analysis, synthesis,* and *evaluation*) have been supplanted to a certain degree in a book titled *A Taxonomy for Learning, Teaching, and Assessing,* by Bloom disciples Lorin Anderson and David Krathwohl. The "new" Bloom replaces the "old" Bloom's six familiar nouns with six verbs (*remembering, understanding, applying, analyzing, evaluating,* and *creating*), culminating in "creativity" rather than "evaluation."

Perhaps the best-known contemporary taxonomy other than Bloom's is that developed by Robert J. Marzano and his associates in a number of contemporary works. This essentially breaks down classroom thinking skills into seven categories: *knowing, organizing, applying, analyzing, generating, integrating,* and *evaluating.* It is interesting to note that Marzano also calls this the "new taxonomy," perhaps also in reference to the "old" Bloom. These taxonomies, both old and new, have enduring value, especially when they serve to remind us that too often the intellectual life of the classroom gets mired at the lowest cognitive levels and that what we desperately need is a proven way of teaching higher-order thinking skills.

In writing this book, we are *not* advocating radical new forms of thinking—or even a radical new nomenclature for thinking skills that already have widely accepted names. Rather, we want to describe a strategy whereby students deliberately practice these traditional skills while discussing a text through a structured process in a controlled setting. Because the setting is controlled, teachers and students work together to create an environment where it is safe to take intellectual risks. This is a naturally slow, but transformative process. In addition, the teacher and students collaboratively challenge and sharpen each other's thinking all along the way.

> *Teachers and students work together to create an environment where it is safe to take intellectual risks.*

How Conversation Helps You Think

The subtitle of this book stresses "using seminars" to teach thinking. The reason is that the tool that we use to understand and manipulate texts, regardless of subject area, is almost always language (or a symbol system like color or number that is similar to a language). The key to teaching thinking, then, is to teach it as one of a cluster of interrelated skills: as part of reading and writing as well as speaking and listening. That is precisely what we propose in this book: to teach thinking through the consistent use of full Paideia Seminar cycles. The Paideia Seminar, which will be described further in the next chapter, is a collaborative intellectual dialogue facilitated with open-ended questions about a text. The literacy cycle of the Seminar includes five steps: pre-seminar reading, preparation for speaking and listening, the dialogue *per se*, a reflection on speaking and listening, and a post-seminar writing assignment. The goal of practicing reading, writing, speaking, and listening skills together is to become more clear, coherent, and sophisticated in our thinking and to contribute to the quality of our lives.

The notion that thinking and language are profoundly related is not a new one. Consider John Locke's explanation from *An Essay Concerning Human Understanding* (1690):

> *Words are sensible signs, necessary for communication of ideas.* Man, though he have great variety of thoughts, and such from which others as well as himself might receive profit and delight; yet they are all within his own breast, invisible and hidden from others, nor can of themselves be made to appear. The comfort and advantage of society not being to be had without communication of thoughts, it was necessary that man should find out some external sensible signs, whereof those invisible ideas, which his thoughts are made up of, might be made known to others. For this purpose nothing was so fit, either for plenty or quickness, as those articulate sounds, which with so much ease and variety he found himself able to make. Thus we may conceive how words, which were by nature so well adapted to that purpose, came to be made use of by men as the signs of their ideas; not by any natural connexion that there is between particular articulate sounds and certain ideas, for then there would be but one language amongst all men; but by a voluntary imposition, whereby such a word is made arbitrarily the mark of such an idea. The use, then, of words, is to be sensible marks of ideas; and the ideas they stand for are their proper and immediate signification.

As Locke notes, part of thinking clearly and coherently is to make explicit the relationship between a word and the idea its represents, so that we can use words to explain and manipulate ideas. For this reason, it is important that we as teachers realize that part of learning to think is language acquisition. The implication is that we must become more literate as scientists, mathematicians, and historians if we are to master these disciplines. As a teacher, you can't coach a student's thinking unless the process is externalized through speaking and writing, and a student can't receive your coaching in turn except by listening and reading. As a result, the more fluent a student becomes as a reader, writer, speaker, and listener, the deeper her or his conceptual understanding—regardless of the subject.

Another interesting perspective regarding thinking in connection to speech is in *Thought and Language* (1934/1986), by the seminal Russian psychologist Lev Vygotsky. He wrote that "thought is not merely expressed in words; it comes into existence through them" (p. 218). As the raw material of thought (images, sounds, incoherent bits of language) rise up through the levels of consciousness, we form them into increasingly more organized structures—almost inevitably linguistic structures. And when we extend this internal process into the external world so that we can share our thoughts, even use them to explain or manipulate the world around us, they become yet more organized. Thus, Vygotsky and his colleagues argued that "thought is not merely expressed in words; it comes into existence through them."

The relationship between thought and word, then, is highly synergistic; thought can find its form only through language, and language devoid of thought is meaningless. Locke addresses this concept:

> First, He that hath words of any language, without distinct ideas in his mind to which he applies them, does, so far as he uses them in discourse, only make a noise without any sense or signification; and how learned so ever he may seem, by the use of hard words or learned terms, is not much more advanced thereby in knowledge, than he would be in learning, who had nothing in his study but the bare titles of books, without possessing the contents of them. Secondly, He that has complex ideas without particular names for them, would be in no better case than a bookseller, who had in his warehouse volumes that lay there unbound, and without titles, which he could therefore make known to others only by showing the loose sheets, and communicate them only by tale (p. 298).

Words without thought are mere sound; thought without words mere phantoms. To teach thinking then, regardless of the subject, we teach the speaking and listening as well as the reading and writing of that subject.

Practical Thinking

At this point, it's appropriate to pause for a clarifying confession. The kind of thinking we are describing here—highly verbal and externalized—is not the only kind of thinking there is. In fact, just as language itself is limited in its ability to illuminate human experience, so is this kind of academic thinking limited. But because our subject is not just thinking skills but the ability to teach those skills in the classroom, we have narrowed our definition of *thought* to one that is both clear and practical.

To illustrate further how we are defining *thought*, let us describe briefly what it is and what it is not—within the boundaries of this discussion. In his intriguing book, *Hare Brain, Tortoise Mind* (wonderfully subtitled "Why Intelligence Increases When You Think Less"), Guy Claxton argues that "roughly speaking, the mind possesses three different processing speeds. The first is faster than thought. Some situations demand an un-selfconscious, instantaneous reaction" (p. 1). We might call this "instantaneous" response instinct or intuition, and Claxton describes it as "a kind of 'intelligence' that works more rapidly than thinking." The second processing speed that Claxton describes "is thought itself: the sort of intelligence which does involve figuring matters out, weighing up the pros and cons, constructing arguments and solving problems." The third processing speed is a "mental register that proceeds more slowly still. It is often less purposeful and clear-cut, more playful, leisurely, or dreamy. In this mode, we are ruminating or mulling things over; being contemplative or meditative" (p. 2).

Although the first and third levels of mental activity that Claxton describes are both fascinating and important,[1] this book is about his second type, the type of thinking that occurs most often in learning an academic discipline. Claxton describes this level of mental processing as a "way of knowing that relies on reason and logic, on deliberate conscious thinking"; it is this type of thinking that involves giving our thoughts structure and clarity through language. In strictly human terms, this highly verbal, external type of processing may not be the most important kind of mental activity that we experience in the course of our lives, but it is the focus of our efforts to teach critical thinking in schools. It is this type of thinking that occurs when a student learns how to explain and manipulate a text rich in the ideas and values of the curriculum. It is this type of thinking that we believe can be taught successfully through careful reading, dialogue, and writing.

In this chapter, we have given a full description of the kind of thinking that we believe can and should be taught in schools—both by saying what that category of thought *is* and what it *is not*. In the next chapter, we will give you a full, working vocabulary to use in teaching thinking through dialogue.

---

1 The whole of this wonderful book is really about Claxton's third type, the "leisurely, apparently aimless, [way] of knowing" that lets the subconscious mind do what it does best—consider the paradoxical problems of life in its own sweet time. We would echo Claxton by arguing that contemplation and meditation have an important role to play in formal education.

Chapter One in Sum

♦ We define thinking as the ability to explain and manipulate a text. By text, we mean a set of interrelated ideas, often represented in a human artifact. Learning to think is the process of explaining and manipulating increasingly complex texts successfully.

2

Coming to Terms: Using Language to Describe Dialogue

"Definitions, like questions and metaphors,
are instruments for thinking."
—Neil Postman

American author and educator Neil Postman says that that the authority of a set of definitions "rests entirely on their usefulness. We use definitions and distort them as suits our purposes." To that end, we would like to provide you with what we believe to be the key definitions for terms we use in this book. For those of you who—like us—could use a "cheat sheet" of the most pertinent terms, we have provided a glossary at the back of this book that summarizes the words and phrases we discuss in the first two chapters.

Teaching Complex Texts

In the previous chapter, we argued that becoming more literate in a discipline is the key to learning to think in that discipline. According to our working definition, learning to think also involves explaining and manipulating the raw material of that discipline, and this usually means explaining and manipulating increasingly complex texts successfully. Thus, learning to think means confronting ideas and values of increasing complexity, a process that is often uncomfortable if it involves confronting a challenge to our understanding of the world. One way to describe this process is the movement from a state of simple mental equilibrium to disequilibrium as new elements and relationships enter our frame of reference. The world becomes more complex and demanding, so we are forced to work harder to explain and manipulate it successfully. Ultimately, a new, more sophisticated and more inclusive explanation emerges, and mental equilibrium is re-established. The Paideia Seminar is designed to evoke precisely this kind of experience through the ambiguity of the text and the force of others' points of view. This is done both to challenge participants to think in broader, more complex ways about the ideas under discussion, and to practice being comfortable with uncertainty.

Comfort with uncertainty is what John Keats famously meant by the phrase "negative capability." In a letter to George and Thomas Keats dated 21 December 1817, the poet wrote:

> I had not a dispute but a disquisition with Dilke, on various subjects; several things dovetailed in my mind, & at once it struck me, what quality went to form a Man of Achievement especially in literature & which Shakespeare possessed so enormously—I mean Negative Capability, that is when man is capable of being in uncertainties, Mysteries, doubts without any irritable reaching after fact & reason. (pp. 41–42)

Curiously, Keats' "disquisition with Dilke" sounds like the sort of full-fledged dialogue between equals that we are describing here, and it resulted in Keats' unique realization. "Men [and Women] of Achievement" are capable of speaking comfortably out of uncertainty, mystery, and doubt. Negative capability is more than listening with an open mind; it involves speaking with a proactive desire to combine elements in new and creative relationships.

Keats makes a point of excluding "any irritable reaching after fact & reason" because negative capability often involves holding even contradictory notions in creative juxtaposition, seeking the larger construct that contains and explains the contradictions. Psychologists tell us that when we are forced to deal with contradictory points of view, especially about a topic that is important to us, we suffer from "cognitive dissonance," another name for Keats' "uncertainties, Mysteries, doubts." In this state, our minds will often reject any information that contradicts our beliefs, causing us to consciously or subconsciously dismiss what we are hearing. Therefore, it requires a truly open mind to practice Keats' negative capability; it is absolutely vital in learning to think successfully about sophisticated topics.

The Paideia Seminar: Roles and Intentions

The Paideia Seminar was originally defined as "teaching by asking questions, by leading discussions, by helping students to raise their minds up from a state of understanding or appreciating less to a state of understanding or appreciating more" (1982). In recent years, we at the National Paideia Center have defined the Paideia Seminar as a *collaborative, intellectual dialogue facilitated with open-ended questions about a text*. This definition (the structure and process) has evolved to capture the practice of thinking through dialogue in conjunction with reading and writing. It is a collaborative process in that the seminar participants work together to construct a deeper understanding of the text—or system—under discussion. It is intellectual in that the purpose of the seminar is to come to grips with the ideas and values in the text, the concepts that lie at the heart of the curriculum.

The role of the seminar facilitator is to provoke discussion through a series of open-ended questions, which take the students deeper into the textual ambiguities where the ideas and values live. We often call these questions "maieutic" as opposed to "Socratic." *Maieutic* is the Greek word for "midwifery," and the term is used here to describe questions that are truly intended to help the students give birth to their own thoughts rather than the thoughts of the facilitator. The facilitator helps the students learn to think and speak for themselves rather than paraphrase the thoughts of the teacher.

The role of the seminar participants is to think seriously about the ideas under discussion, to share their thoughts by making statements and asking questions, and to listen with an open mind to the statements of others. Thus, the Paideia Seminar is designed to enhance both the intellectual (or thinking) skills as well as the social (or communication) skills of the participants through consistent, deliberate practice.

Keeping this in mind, the word *understanding* means quite explicitly the result of intellectual striving, or focused, structured thinking. When engaged in a seminar, the individual participant is witness both to the thinking process of other individuals and to the collective thinking process of the group. Both of these can serve as educative models for increasingly clear, coherent, sophisticated thinking.

> **When engaged in a seminar, the individual participant is witness both to the thinking process of other individuals and to the collective thinking process of the group.**

The intention of Paideia Seminar practice is to develop more fluency in the language that is in use as well as the willingness to experience the cognitive dissonance that comes from considering multiple, even contradictory points of view. The various stages of the cycle are designed to teach *fluency*—mastery in the flow of language—while the entire process is meant to guide students through intellectual disequilibrium to a more sophisticated understanding that lies beyond.

Our goal is thinking that is *clear*, *coherent*, and *sophisticated*. We essentially mean spoken and written statements with these qualities:

♦ *clarity* in articulating and explaining a point so that it can be correctly understood by auditor or reader at first exposure

♦ enough *coherence* so that the connection between various points make sense in relation to each other

◆ *sophistication* in that a point is expanded upon by synthesizing variables and acknowledging one's own personal bias

Our argument in this book is built on the assumption that practice in reading, speaking, listening, and writing about increasingly complex texts leads to this kind of thinking. We will focus primarily on speaking and listening as forms of thinking, because they so desperately need our attention now.

Chapter Two in Sum

◆ We introduce a strategy—the Paideia Seminar—whereby students deliberately practice thinking skills while discussing a text through a structured process in a controlled setting. The Paideia Seminar nurtures basic speaking and listening as well as reading and writing skills—the literacy skills that make up thinking.

◆ We discuss the following terms:

  ◆ *thinking* (as it should be taught in school)

  ◆ *mental equilibrium* and *disequilibrium*

  ◆ *negative capability*

  ◆ *cognitive dissonance*

  ◆ *maieutic* and *Socratic questions*

  ◆ *understanding*

  ◆ *fluency*

We will use those terms throughout the book as we illuminate how to teach thinking through seminar dialogue.

The goal of teaching thinking through dialogue is student thinking that is more *clear, coherent,* and *sophisticated.* These and other key terms are also defined in the glossary beginning on page 162.

3

The Paideia Seminar in Action

"The greatest compliment that was ever paid me was when one asked me what I thought, and attended to my answer."
—Henry David Thoreau

Some years ago, we visited a magnet school in Chicago that was defined in part by its dedication to the Paideia Program and in particular, the Paideia Seminar.[1] As we visited classrooms that day, we asked students to describe their experience in seminar, and they told us about especially memorable texts and discussions. It was obvious from their enthusiasm that they took great pride in their ability to discuss big ideas. When we walked into one sixth-grade classroom, a girl turned the tables on us and started to ask us questions. "What caused *you* to become interested in seminar in the first place?" Terry replied that he had long been moved by the thrill that comes when we learn something for the first time. "It doesn't matter how many others have had the same thought before; when you experience an idea for the first time, it's as if it's being born inside your head." Students were nodding, many smiling in recognition of this experience. Terry added, "It's like a flash of lightning, isn't it, sudden and bright, and it seems to me that seminar is the one place in school where the most lightning strikes." One student suddenly called out without raising his hand: "You got that right!"

One of the reasons that cognitive lightning strikes so often during seminar discussion is that, by definition, Paideia Seminars feature the discussion of significant ideas and values—evocative, often profound ideas and values. (See Appendix A for further discussion of this element and a list of sug-

---

1 This experience is described in more detail in "Learn to Care, Care to Learn" (*Educational Leadership*, September 2002).

gested ideas and values.) When we define the seminar as "a collaborative, intellectual dialogue facilitated with open-ended questions about a text," the word *intellectual* is intended to denote this important quality. The fact that a seminar is conducted in response to open-ended questions also supports this attribute, because open-ended questions evoke a variety of right answers; taken together, these provide multiple perspectives on an idea, leading ultimately to more sophisticated understanding.

Thinking About Infinity: An Elementary Math Seminar

To further illustrate the intellectual power of seminar discussion, we invite you to visit a third-grade classroom in a North Carolina school of several years ago. The school was committed to the Paideia Program, and all students participated in a school-wide seminar every other week. Let's call the school Spring Garden Elementary. On this particular day, the local legislative contingent was scheduled to visit the school to see a Paideia Seminar in action. The seminar text for grades three to five on that day was an etching by Dutch artist M.C. Escher titled the *Mobius Strip*. We were especially excited because we had designed the seminar plan to investigate the idea of *infinity*—both as a mathematical concept and as an idea in general. In addition, we anticipated discussing other big ideas, such as *art*, *form*, *mathematics*, and *symbol*.

Due to teacher absences, we were both leading seminars that day, and so we both had the opportunity to lead a student discussion with the seminar plan we had helped to create. Part of the pre-seminar content process involved displaying a definition of a Mobius Strip:

> *The Mobius Strip or Mobius Band is an interesting geometric figure (that looks like a figure 8), which can be formed by giving a strip of paper a half turn and joining the two ends together.*

Prior to the seminar, we discussed this definition in some detail and shared some background information on Escher. Then, we distributed long ribbons of chart paper (one-inch wide by twenty-four-inches long) to the students so that each could create a Mobius Strip of his or her own. (See the sample Mobius strip in Figure 3.1, page 14.) Once the figures were secured end-to-end with clear tape, the students laid their own creations aside and took up the image as their seminar text.

After we went through the typical pre-seminar process exercises, during which students chose personal process goals, we began the discussion itself. The opening question was: "Where does the strip begin (or end)?" Each student was given the opportunity to either point to or describe where he or she thought the strip started and explain why.

Figure 3.1. Sample Mobius Strip

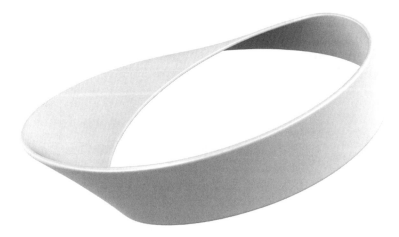

The 25 or so nine- and ten-year-old kids in Terry's seminar gave a variety of answers. Two said there was no beginning or end. The strip was "endless," another said, which puzzled some of the students, including a girl named Emma. "How can something be endless?" she asked.

Terry redirected the discussion at this point by asking the students to remember the word *endless*, and promising that they would return to the idea later in their discussion. He then asked the students why they thought Escher chose to have ants crawling on his version of the Mobius Strip. "Why ants?" Several silly answers followed, including the notion that he could have used alligators...or bears. One boy said, quite happily, "Butterflies. He could have had butterflies crawling around and around."

"But they would have flown away," a boy named Joshua said. "Once they got bored from crawling, they would have flown away."

The first boy looked nonplussed for a minute but then shrugged. "You're right. Ants don't get bored. I've watched them out on the playground, and they go on forever."

"That's right," Joshua added. "Even if you stomp on some of the ants, the rest of 'em keep right on going."

Most of the students seemed to agree that the ants were a good idea. A bear would have torn up the strip and run away. An alligator would have eaten the strip and then eaten Escher. (Joshua liked the idea of the bear eating Escher.) But ants were the best. "Because they go on forever," Emma said, echoing Joshua's earlier words.

At this point, Terry asked the students to each pick an ant and, with a finger, trace the path that one particular ant would take around the strip, just to see where it would end up. The boys and girls liked this exercise because it meant they got to touch the text and play with it. One girl asked if she could use a crayon to trace an ant's path, and Terry nodded. Several got out crayons or pencils.

There followed universal surprise. "My ant goes all around and comes back to the same exact place!" cried Nathan, the smallest boy in the class. "Mine too," said the girl beside him, beaming at Nathan.

"Is that what the rest of you think?" Terry asked.

Most nodded or said yes.

"Then, I want you to look closely. How many sides does the Mobius Strip actually have?"

There were shouts of "one" and "no, it's two."

"Is it one or is it two? Look again."

While the students were retracing the paths of their respective ants and examining the text in great detail, three state legislators escorted by the school principal came into the room. The legislators seemed vaguely disappointed that the students were so engrossed in their work that they barely even bothered to look up.

The principal gave the legislators copies of the text as they settled in to watch the seminar. "What have you decided?" Terry asked the students. "Is it one or two?"

There were renewed arguments for both answers, with both sides giving reasons. Then Nathan said, "Maybe it's both. Maybe it's magic or something like that. But really it's both one and two."

Terry made a note to suggest that this teacher consider adding the word *paradox* to the vocabulary list for this class. They were certainly ready for it. Then he took the next step in the seminar plan. He asked for the students' attention and said, "In math there is an idea called *infinity*. Earlier, one of you said the Mobius Strip was *endless*. Later in our seminar, Joshua said the ants went on *forever*. Can you use these words to define what we mean when we say that something is infinite?"

After a moment, Emma spoke up. "I think that *infinite* means something like 'endless numbers.' In our math book last year, there were number lines that ended in arrows, and the teacher said that meant they kept going."

"Right on off the page," another girl added helpfully.

"Maybe the numbers went on forever, like the ants," Joshua offered.

There was more discussion of number lines, including number lines that went on forever in both directions, which was why we had to have negative numbers.

"So we're agreed then?" Terry asked, being careful to use the students' words. "*Infinite* means something that goes on forever, without an end."

The students nodded.

Terry went on. "If you turn the Mobius Strip on its side so that it's lying down, it looks like the symbol that mathematicians use for infinity. Do you think the Mobius Strip is a good symbol for infinity? Why or why not?"

Terry was glad to see that the legislators were finally starting to pay attention to what the students were saying. Two of the three were even examining their texts closely as they listened, tracing the path of the ants on the Mobius Strip. The students, who at this point were far ahead of the legislators in their deliberations, agreed that they thought the Mobius Strip was the perfect symbol for infinity, because it went on forever without running off the page.

Before letting the discussion go too far (the principal was looking at her watch, and one of the legislators was getting restless), Terry asked one more core question. "Why do you think we need a symbol for an idea like the infinite?"

There was a long pause, a pause that seemed to stretch on and on. The principal stepped toward the door, and two of the legislators started to get up to go, but the third raised her hand to stop them. The pause stretched on.

"Some ideas are too big," Nathan whispered, and then repeated himself more loudly. "Some ideas are too big for us to even hold in our minds….We need the idea in order to explain something or understand something, but it's too big to put down on a piece of paper as it is."

"Like the number line with the arrow on the end," Emma whispered.

Nathan nodded. "Yeah. Like the number line. So if an idea is too big to put down on a piece of paper, we need a symbol, something we can draw on a piece of paper, to represent it. That way we can talk about it or write about it even though it's a lot bigger than we are."

The other students stared at Nathan. Not all understood, but many of them began to nod. The much larger girl who sat beside Nathan reached over to pat him on the shoulder. "Yup," she said. "I agree with Nathan. Big ideas need symbols to represent them."

Even the third legislator was ready to go now. She smiled at Nathan and then turned to wink at Terry, the facilitator. The principal ushered the three out of the room, pushing them on, with the day's schedule in hand.

Once the legislators were out of the room, Terry asked the closing question of the seminar: "What kinds of things can you think of that are infinite?"

"The sky," Emma said. "The sky is endless…."

The post-seminar writing assignment for this seminar was for students to choose three things they thought were infinite and write them in a repeating pattern on "both" sides of the strip of paper from their pre-seminar attempts to make a Mobius Strip. Emma, for example, wrote the words *sky*, *sun*, and *moon* on her ribbon of paper. Then Terry and a parent volunteer helped each student carefully twist and connect his or her strip, so that each had a personal record of the "infinite" in the form of a Mobius Strip. These were displayed in the class for a week before being taken home to share.

Literacy Skills and Big Ideas

In introducing the Common Core State Standards (CCSS) in 2010, Vicki Phillips and Carina Wong of the Bill and Melinda Gates Foundation wrote that the foundation was advocating for the CCSS, because "the evidence supports the need for students to have certain skills as they move into college." Of the four skills that Phillips and Wong cited, at least three are directly related to seminar dialogue, but in this context, the first skill they list leaps off the page: "Academic skills and content that are basic but also *encompass big ideas in the disciplines*" (p. 38, emphasis added). In other words, it's time we brought conceptual understanding back onto center stage in our classrooms. The second skill—"Cognitive skills, such as problem solving, collaboration, and academic risk taking"—suggests how we might best reintroduce big ideas into the curriculum and reinforces our call for consistent use of formal classroom discussion.

Perhaps the most remarkable thing about seminars in elementary school is that the students make great developmental strides in the most natural and unaffected ways. Nathan's classmates didn't laugh in embarrassment or ridicule him when he announced that some ideas were too big to hold in our minds or even represent on a sheet of paper. They listened, even when they didn't understand, and they struggled to go with him when the lightning flashed inside his mind. Later in school—middle school, high school, and college—the social lives of students can inhibit their native curiosity, even their intellectual elasticity. Indeed, we would argue that part of the function of seminar dialogue is to keep the sense of intellectual wonder alive in schools. Nathan and his classmates didn't just define *infinity*; they also exemplified the Paideia Seminar by demonstrating open-minded curiosity in response to complex, paradoxical ideas. This is the state of mind that the Paideia Seminar is designed to encourage and enhance.

Chapter Three in Sum

The Paideia Seminar is a collaborative, intellectual dialogue facilitated with open-ended questions about a text. The seminar is designed to teach conceptual understanding of the complex ideas and values that give meaning to the curriculum.

4

Introducing Speaking and Listening Skills

*"It is impossible to acquire skill in conversation—
in talk or discussion—without learning how to speak
and how to listen well."*

—Mortimer Adler

It is not uncommon, when we spend the day working with a group of teachers, for someone in the room to suddenly exclaim (usually after either being in a seminar or seeing one demonstrated with students): "Oh, I get it now. This really is about giving kids the opportunity to talk about ideas. . . . I'm sure that's great for some kids, but it'll never work with my third period." Or with the kids in our average classes." Or with these children from the inner city." Or with rural kids." As we discuss it further, what emerges is that many teachers assume that their students either have the inherent ability to carry on a civil conversation or they don't. Which brings us to perhaps the single most common misconception about speaking and listening skills: They are a function of personality or early socialization, but not education. Unlike reading and writing, which seem to fall within the province of the classroom, our speaking and listening habits are formed elsewhere and there is little we can do about it—either as individuals or as teachers. We are arguing that, just as with reading and writing, speaking and listening are learned behaviors that must be taught. Thus, what we really mean when we say that a group of participants can't "do seminars" is that no one has ever taken the time to break down the process and show them how.

If you were to observe a first or second seminar with a group of inexperienced participants (even adults), you might observe a lot of discouraging behavior. Early seminars with any group tend to showcase some if not all of the following characteristics:

- ◆ participants who dominate while many individuals passively observe (or mentally check out)
- ◆ participants who don't make eye contact with the person who is speaking
- ◆ participants who engage in "sidebar" conversations
- ◆ participants who miss key points, either in the text or in the comments of others
- ◆ participants who offer barely audible comments
- ◆ participants who make unrelated or repetitive points
- ◆ participants who draw their conclusions about the ideas under discussion from a single perspective
- ◆ participants who don't ask questions or build on earlier statements

All of these behaviors limit thinking and communication and restrict the potential for conceptual understanding of both the individual and the group. Yet, they are perfectly familiar in conversations of all kinds, both formal and informal.

Faced with behaviors like these, it is easy to see why we often give up on teaching a classroom full of students to speak and listen thoughtfully. Indeed, as Mortimer Adler points out in the Prologue to his 1983 book *How to Speak How to Listen*, what makes this lack of attention "so amazing and extraordinary is the fact that the two generally untaught skills, speaking and listening, are much more difficult to acquire and more difficult to teach than the parallel skills of writing and reading" (p. 5). Part of the reason why they are so difficult to teach is because, as Adler points out, they "are transient and fleeting," and "a given performance, once it is given, cannot be improved" (p. 9).

As daunting as the task may be, learning to speak and listen well is truly basic—fundamental to learning any subject and fundamental to learning how to think. The goal of any effective school, then, is to help everyone involved (including the adults) practice the habits of skillful speaking and listening. In this chapter, we are going to examine a variety of examples in which facilitators are faced with exactly the kinds of counterproductive behaviors described above and, even more to the point, what they do to coach individual and group behaviors toward meaningful dialogue.

Reaching All Students During the Seminar

The single, most common question asked by facilitators who are learning to lead seminars is how to get the dominant to talk less and the reticent to talk more. In some ways, this is the quintessential problem—both because it is so common and also because it serves to introduce the pre- and post-seminar process sessions where good facilitators do most of their coaching. During a recent visit we made to an urban middle school, a teacher proudly shared with us her seminar portfolio, in which she had collected the text, plan, map, and reflection notes for each of the three seminars she had led up to that point in the school year. (By "map" we mean a seating-chart type format where the facilitator takes notes on talk turns, key ideas, and various other details.) She used the three seminar maps to point out what most troubled her—that the same five students had dominated every discussion. While those five students averaged eight talk turns each, the rest of the class barely spoke at all. Although this is an extreme example, it clearly illustrates the problem. When we are first learning to participate in a formal discussion, our natural preferences tend to take over, and this lasts until our old habits are replaced by new ones. When this teacher (at our request) repeated her question in front of the whole faculty, we explained to the group that if a given student is naturally a confident speaker and willingly takes the lead in seminar discussion, the goal is not merely to get that student to be quiet; rather, the goal is to help her or him learn to invite others in and to listen with equal intensity. If another student is naturally more withdrawn and all but refuses to speak out even when interested in the discussion, then the goal is to help that student gain the confidence to voice her or his thoughts openly. In each case, it is about learning new skills to complement existing ones.

We have learned over the years that the best way to do this is to help participants become aware of both their strengths and weaknesses in thoughtful dialogue. We also give them clear strategies for practicing particular skills.

Just as beginning readers learn new reading strategies, beginning seminar participants learn new speaking and listening strategies.

Just as beginning readers learn new reading strategies, beginning seminar participants learn new speaking and listening strategies. As a result, we have added pre- and post-seminar process steps to each seminar plan that we develop. During these steps, students assign themselves specific process speaking and listening goals (before the seminar) and then assess their own progress (afterward). During the day we spent with this teacher and her colleagues, we demonstrated these steps during a faculty seminar that we led on Francis Bacon's essay "Of Studies." During the pre-seminar process work, we offered the teachers the following options for their personal process goals:

- Speak at least three times.
- Agree or disagree with someone else in detail.
- Ask a question.
- Keep an open mind.

The first two options are designed to help less talkative participants speak out and with purpose. The third and fourth are designed to help participants focus on listening with purpose.

Our response, therefore, to the candid middle school teacher who was concerned that her seminars thus far were dominated by the same few participants was to show her how to create both group and personal process goals that speak directly to this dynamic. After the faculty seminar we led that day, we demonstrated the post-seminar self-assessment process that serves to emphasize the same goals. First, as an entire group, we discussed our relative success with understanding the text more deeply. The teachers laughed and freely admitted that they had hated the text to begin with because they couldn't make sense of it, but as time went on and they began to grasp its meaning, they grew more and more willing to discuss it openly, even asking candid questions about passages they didn't understand. We talked about the value of discussing an ambiguous or even mystifying text. We then had them write a brief, personal self-assessment about their personal goals, stressing complete candor. Once they had spent almost five minutes writing, we asked volunteers to share what they had learned. In the discussion that followed, we stressed that the talkers were learning to listen while the listeners were learning to share their ideas. We ended the post-seminar process session by having the teachers set personal goals for the next faculty seminar based on their performance that day.

The teachers grasped that the pre- and post-seminar process sessions were the intervals in the seminar cycle when they could and should do the majority of their skills-coaching participation—including the coaching of listening skills. Perhaps all listening skills begin with the ability to look directly at the person who is speaking and focus on her or his words. When first learning to participate, young children in particular struggle to maintain eye contact with the speaker because they are so easily distracted. One of the most effective elementary seminar leaders we know (call her Ms. Simmons) describes how each year she introduces a new group of third graders to seminar practice. In the beginning, they find it all but impossible to focus on the speaker for more than a few moments at a time, and often there are three or four children speaking or whispering at once.

In response, Ms. Simmons typically does two things. First, at the beginning of the year, she divides her class in half for seminar: She lets half the class read, draw, or circulate through instructional centers (often having to do with the seminar text) while she leads the seminar discussion with the other half; and then she reverses the groups, so that she can then lead the discussion with the second group of students. This strategy allows her to hold early seminar discussions with ten or twelve students rather than twenty plus, making it easier for her seven-year-olds to focus on the speaker. From the beginning, however, she is clear that she expects her students to mature so that they will be holding whole-class seminars by the end of the year. Along the way, Ms. Simmons also teaches her students through role play in a game she calls "Show Me Listening." This game encourages anyone in the seminar circle who is speaking to know that others really are paying attention. Ms. Simmons constantly tells her students:

> It's not enough for you just to listen. You have to let your friend who is speaking know you are listening. You have to *show* them by looking directly at them, by nodding and by asking them questions nicely when you don't understand.

During her pre-seminar process work, Ms. Simmons selects a student to read part of the seminar text aloud and has the other students in the circle demonstrate their listening while she watches, coaching and encouraging. In this way, she turns what might seem like a silent, passive activity into a dramatic gesture that she can observe and coach. In the beginning, she laughingly admits, her students "over act" listening in sometimes hilarious ways, but before long, they settle down into the habit of looking directly at the speaker and outgrow the need to have whispered sidebar conversations or raise their hands to speak.

Coaching Students to Speak Up

Just as pre- and post-seminar process sessions provide the facilitator with the opportunity to coach listening skills, they also provide the opportunity to coach discrete speaking skills. As simply looking at the speaker and focusing on his or her words is the beginning of skillful listening, so actually speaking up—loudly and clearly—is the beginning of skillful speaking. One of the first challenges faced by any seminar leader is to get all, or at least most, of her participants freely sharing their ideas. Ms. Simmons' second graders will again serve to provide a case study. At the beginning of each year, not only does she struggle to get them to focus on the speaker, but she also struggles to get them to speak out so that they *can* be heard. Her goal, as stated in her own teaching portfolio, is to lead a whole-group seminar by the end of each school year in which every single student voluntarily speaks a few times. She is quick to point out, however, that this is not the end goal but rather the means to an end, which is thoughtful, connected discussion.

Ms. Simmons adopts a number of strategies to get her kids talking. In addition to coaching the reticent children to choose individual process goals that involve speaking, she also has them practice speaking in the same way that she has them role play listening. She does this by first having them take turns reading the seminar text out loud in the seminar circle, coaching them to speak loudly and clearly while they read. She then has the entire class work at a writing center in her classroom to draft a written response to a core question she intends to ask in the seminar, so that when the time comes, she can call on certain quiet students to read their response to the question—again stressing that they do so loudly and clearly. Finally, as the year progresses, and it becomes increasingly clear who among her students is having the most trouble expressing themselves in seminar, she begins to differentiate even more.

> By mid-year, I feel like I know who struggles most with talking and why they struggle. My favorite strategy is to talk with them individually in advance of the seminar and give them hints about questions I intend to ask, so that they can practice saying an answer and even practice delivering it to me or to a few other students before having to speak out in front of the whole class. Over time, it's a matter of working up the courage to speak comfortably before larger and larger groups of people. And always, always I emphasize how important what they have to say is to all of us. "We can't completely understand the story until we've heard from everyone"—I must say that ten times a day leading up to a seminar.

It is important to note that Ms. Simmons emphasizes learning to speak comfortably, both for the sake of the individual student who is struggling to master the skill and also for the other students, who can benefit from what the reluctant student has to say.

The Rough Drafts of Thoughts

As seminar participants of all ages begin to speak up, they often make repetitive or disconnected statements. In other words, the fact that participants are learning to talk doesn't guarantee that they have learned to think through what they are saying. This lack of coherence tends to reveal itself in two ways. One, they offer a series of unrelated comments rather than connecting what they have to say to earlier comments or questions. Two, participants digress during the course of the seminar, drifting further and further away from the text and its ideas.[1] Both of these phenomena are symptomatic

---

1 One of the reasons that seminar participants resist talking about the text is that they don't feel they understand it initially. Their reluctance is often a reading problem as well as a speaking problem, and teachers should be careful to make sure that they have led students through

of participants who are not yet willing—or able—to build more sophisticated responses to the seminar text and questions. A middle school language arts teacher that we work with (call him Colonel Bird since he is a retired military officer) compares the discussion to listening to your radio when it's set on "scan."

> You get a whole series of disconnected comments. Not just discon- nected from the text but also from each other—a few seconds of jazz followed by a few seconds of rock followed by a few seconds of clas- sical and so on. A few of the comments are reasonably insightful but most are fairly simple minded, even naïve, responses.

What Colonel Bird doesn't say but could is that his students' comments are relatively simple because in most instances they represent a first response, something like the rough draft of a thought. The students are willing, even anxious, to talk, but they are so focused on their own initial reaction to the text that they haven't bothered to put their thoughts in any sort of context. The result is a staccato series of isolated comments.

With our help, Colonel Bird has developed a series of strategies for help- ing students anchor their comments to the seminar text and at least recognize how their comments fit in relation to what's already been said. Early in the year, he often sets as the group goal for participants to refer to the text every time they speak; and not just to refer to the text, but also to "cite chapter and verse," meaning to direct the seminar circle to a specific passage in the text before offering a comment. When his students complain that they don't un- derstand the text well enough to talk about it, he replies, "then ask a specific question about a specific passage. Let's help each other figure out what we think the text is saying." He also keeps "refer to the text" on his list of per- sonal process goals, so he can direct those students who tend most often to digress back to that strategy as an individual goal.

Encouraging Differences of Opinion

Early in the year, Colonel Bird stresses that part of his pre-seminar pro- cess instructions have to do with agreeing and disagreeing graciously. "In my pre-seminar script, I have these words highlighted," he admits, "so I don't forget to say them."

> We will practice using others' names and paraphrasing what we hear others saying. We will agree and disagree in a courteous, thoughtful manner.

---

at least one deliberate reading strategy with regards to a text they hope for them to discuss successfully.

For example, when another participant (Sam for example) says something you like, the best response is to say "I agree with Sam because…." And what comes after the "because" is the important part because that's the connection between ideas.

By the same token, when someone says something you dislike, you don't laugh at them or call them names. You say "I disagree with Sam because…." And once again, you stress what Sam said that you disagree with and why. It's not personal, it's about contrasting ideas.

What Colonel Bird is doing is creating the atmosphere wherein it is not just all right to disagree; it is expected and even applauded. When students recognize what someone else has said, they are beginning to create a collaborative climate in which it will be easier to recognize and integrate multiple perspectives.

> *When students recognize what someone else has said, they are beginning to create a collaborative climate in which it will be easier to recognize and integrate multiple perspectives.*

The ability to base conclusions on multiple perspectives is not something that comes naturally to most students; it is a function of both their listening and speaking skills. They first have to hear and comprehend one or more points of view different from their own and then struggle to articulate what a more comprehensive perspective might sound like. The first step involves listening and the second, speaking. This ability requires a level of sophistication beyond merely agreeing or disagreeing with a previous comment; it involves placing two or more comments in creative juxtaposition, which is the goal of any successful seminar discussion. To illustrate this process, let us describe a demonstration seminar we once led in a high school American history class. The seminar was on "The New Colossus" by Emma Lazarus, the sonnet inscribed on the base of the Statue of Liberty.

> *Not like the brazen giant of Greek fame,*
> *With conquering limbs astride from land to land;*
> *Here at our sea-washed, sunset gates shall stand*
> *A mighty woman with a torch, whose flame*
> *Is the imprisoned lightning, and her name*
> *Mother of Exiles. From her beacon-hand*
> *Glows world-wide welcome; her mild eyes command*
> *The air-bridged harbor that twin cities frame.*
> *"Keep ancient lands, your storied pomp!" cries she*
> *With silent lips. "Give me your tired, your poor,*
> *Your huddled masses yearning to breathe free,*
> *The wretched refuse of your teeming shore.*

Send these, the homeless, tempest-tost to me,
I lift my lamp beside the golden door!"

This seminar had to do with the history of immigration in the United States, but very quickly it became about contemporary controversies surrounding immigration, especially having to do with the growing number of undocumented Hispanics in the community. The Hispanic students in the seminar freely quoted Emma Lazarus' poem to defend a more open policy, while several Anglo students called for the deportation of any "illegals." The seminar became increasingly emotional, and many of the students grew steadily more entrenched in their positions as the opposing camps began to raise their voices at each other. We eventually calmed the participants by repeatedly asking them to return to the poem itself as a way of practicing historical thinking, but even after the seminar there were hard words and hard stares between several students. Far too many students had become stuck in their original perspectives and were refusing to recognize any other points of view. This is a perfect example of how the seminar challenges participants to deal with negative capability.

The classroom teacher for whom we were demonstrating the seminar captured the dilemma perfectly when she remarked afterwards that "it seems like my students only become more narrow-minded when presented with an opposing point of view." The ability to recognize and even appreciate a different perspective is a hard one for inexperienced teachers to coach, especially when the topic under discussion has to do with race, religion, politics, or other emotionally charged issues. We explained that one way to confront this problem is to discuss a text that has directly to do with the dangers of partisanship; in this case, we recommended an excerpt from John Stuart Mill's *On Liberty*. Even more to the point, we recommended having students identify their positions on a controversial issue before the seminar and then pair them up with seminar partners who believed differently. Prior to the seminar, pairs of students would practice explaining their positions calmly and clearly to each other and then let each student summarize his or her partner's position for the whole group. We suggested using the phrase we learned from Swedish researcher Ann Pihlgren: "to take a distance from thy self." This may feel like a form of role-playing—the process of articulating an opposing point of view under controlled circumstances or responding from an objective viewpoint. A few weeks later, the teacher whose class had gotten so emotional over "The New Colossus" led her students through this role-playing exercise before tackling an equally controversial text. This time, she reported, they were able to remain more objective and discuss opposing points of view with relative calm.

Faculty Seminars

Once the seminar participants have gained enough experience to recognize and even appreciate differing points of view, they are ready to begin inviting a variety of perspectives into the discussion by asking genuine questions and even remarking upon the connections they discover. We advocate strongly that school faculties (as well as other groups of professionals) involved in leading seminars practice what they preach by participating in regular adult seminars. This lets them experience what their students are experiencing during seminar discussion, and thus makes them more effective seminar leaders. It also gives them the opportunity to continue developing their own speaking and listening skills.

A few years ago, we were involved with faculty members who were new to the school and didn't know each other well at all. Initially, they were very reluctant to ask each other questions during our seminar discussions, even when we listed "asking genuine questions" as a group or individual process goal.

As they became increasingly comfortable with each other—and as we continued to emphasize trust as part of the seminar culture—they slowly began to evolve. In one evocative moment during a seminar on a short story titled "Mary" by Maya Angelou (actually, an excerpt from *I Know Why the Caged Bird Sings*), a single exchange opened this group to the potential of dialogue. We had again listed "Ask at least one genuine question" as an option for a personal process goal, and part way through the seminar, a young teacher spoke up.

> Ms. Smith: I would like to *ask* (with a humorous glance at the facilitator to be sure it was recorded as a question) my colleagues if any of you ever had to fight for your name the way the character in this story did?

There was a long, somewhat awkward pause, before a very distinguished African American woman reached out to tap the name tent in front of her.

> Ms. Jones: This is not my name…. It says "Ella" on there, I know, but that's not what my mother named me. She named me Jonquell—J-o-n-q-u-e-l-l—because that's how she thought you spelled the flower and because my grandfather's name was John. I loved my name but when I went to school, the white ladies there—no offense—said they couldn't understand what I was saying and they wouldn't let me spell it out.

By this point, Ms. Jones had tears in her eyes, as did a number of other participants.

Those ladies in that school renamed me Ella and made me answer to it, and I've been Ella ever since. It even says "Ella" on my driver's license. Until now. Until (with a nod to Ms. Smith) Nancy asked and I thought I could say.

She picked up her name tent, folded it inside out, and began purposefully to rewrite her name.

Ms. Smith: I hate to ask this, but in what ways do you think we do something like that to our own students?

Mr. James: Every time we call Jesus Mendez "Gee-sus" and the kids all laugh. Every time we joke because some child's name is spelled in a way that is different or funny. Every time we prejudge a child because of a name. I do it. Maybe we all do it.

Two questions from a young, perhaps naïve teacher—that's all it took to jump start a dialogue and to begin bringing a faculty, unaccustomed to genuine dialogue, closer together in understanding. As several said in their post-seminar reflections, not only did they develop a better understanding of the ideas represented by the story, but they understood themselves and each other better.

What Ms. Smith did quite naturally by asking her follow-up question ("In what ways do you think we do something similar to our students?"), good seminar facilitators learn to do deliberately. They address follow-up questions to the entire group, thereby asking them to discuss what has already been said but at greater depth. In addition, they pose questions that ask participants to juxtapose multiple points of view, such as these:

- Some of you say you are more like the lion; some say more like the mouse. How are the lion and the mouse alike? How are they different?

- You have identified these two events in the story as important. How would you say they are related?

- Of the twelve principles listed here, we have been focusing on the last three. Why do you think the authors grouped them together?

These questions—based on the elements from the text that the students have identified—ask the participants to combine multiple perspectives in new ways, quite probably in ways the students themselves hadn't considered before. By asking these and similar questions, the seminar facilitator is coaching her students' speaking skills and in doing so, she is also coaching their thinking skills, especially analysis—the key to other higher-order thinking skills.

The result is that a group of seminar participants—regardless of their age—can and do learn how to participate in formal seminar discussion through practice. They gain measurable skill in speaking and listening just as they do in the complementary skills of reading and writing. Even more to the point, as they are learning to speak and listen, they are also learning to think.

In the first chapter of this book, we defined *thinking* as the ability to explain and manipulate a text. By *text*, we said we meant a set of interrelated elements, often represented in a human artifact. And by the phrase, *learning to think*, we meant the process of explaining and manipulating increasingly complex texts successfully. We have in this chapter shown a number of examples of seminar facilitators struggling to teach their seminar groups how to speak and listen proficiently in relation to a text—thereby teaching them how to explain and manipulate that text. What we have shown you here are human beings from six to sixty years old learning to think with more clarity, coherence, and sophistication about a range of ideas. (For those who are classroom teachers, it is worth pointing out that the school-age seminar participants are also learning to think about language arts, history, math, and science.)

Finally, of course, the ability to think and communicate about ideas has even more value in life after graduation—where the tests are much harder and the stakes much higher—than it does in the classroom. Citizenship, a good life, and a decent livelihood are dependent on communication and thinking. For that reason, we continue to stress that learning to read, write, speak, listen, and … think is a lifelong quest, what Robert Maynard Hutchins called the "interminable liberal education" (p. 52). The development of the mind is so important that the struggle for mere proficiency (as portrayed in this chapter) is never enough.

Chapter Four in Sum

We argue that speaking and listening (like reading and writing) are not a function of personality but rather learned skills that must be taught in school. Practicing these four skills in concert is the only way we have to consistently teach clear, coherent, and sophisticated thinking in our classrooms.

Beginning seminars (regardless of the age of the participants) are characterized by some if not all of the following characteristics:

- participants who dominate while many individuals passively observe

- participants who don't make eye contact with the person who is speaking

- ♦ participants who engage in sidebar conversations
- ♦ participants who miss key points, either in the text or in the comments of others
- ♦ participants who offer barely audible comments
- ♦ participants who make unrelated or repetitive points
- ♦ participants who draw their conclusions about the ideas under discussion from a single perspective
- ♦ participants who don't ask questions or build on earlier comments

During pre- and post-seminar process sessions, teachers coach speaking and listening skills by having students identify and practice specific behaviors designed to overcome these characteristics.

5

Mastering Speaking and Listening Skills

"Reading maketh a full man;
conference a ready man;
and writing an exact man."
—Francis Bacon

Often when we meet with teachers who have had some experience leading seminars, someone will invariably ask a version of the following question:

"Oh, come on, Laura (or Terry), be honest. Isn't the seminar really about teaching social skills?"

And we'll say, "Yes."

And then someone else will say something like, "Whoa, wait a minute. A little while ago, you said it was about thinking skills!"

"Yes."

"Which is it? Thinking skills or social skills?"

"Yes."

The Evolution of Literacy Skills

Social skills are thinking skills. This is another way of saying that learning to speak and listen about math is learning to *think* about math (or language or history or science). As our students get older and more sophisticated, they should naturally become aware of their growing skills in speaking and listening just as they become more aware of their own thinking processes.

This growing self-awareness doesn't mean that students have mastered all the speaking and listening skills they will need in life; on the contrary, the more one learns, the more there is to learn. After several years of consistent seminar experience, it is not unusual for a group of students to exhibit many of the following attributes (individually and collectively):

- ◆ dialogue that is more nearly balanced in terms of the talkative and the quiet participants

- ◆ dialogue in which most participants look at the person speaking and rarely talk while another is speaking

- ◆ participants yielding to another as a way of sharing talk time

- ◆ participants making clear and accurate statements, using generally appropriate pace, volume, vocabulary, and grammar

- ◆ participants taking notes either on the text or on the comments of others

- ◆ participants offering relevant and detailed comments in terms of sequence, purpose, and point of view

- ◆ participants referring regularly to the text or another relevant source

- ◆ participants considering another point of view while acknowledging their own bias

- ◆ participants asking authentic questions

- ◆ participants paraphrasing the comments of others

Were you to first observe a completely inexperienced group of seminar participants and then revisit that same group some time later, you would be struck by their evolution—both individually and collectively. Even as they exhibited the characteristics listed above, however, it would be obvious that there was still room for improvement.

After several years of continuous seminar practice, students should still be focused on developing their skills—even as the content they are studying is becoming more and more complex. In fact, it is their steadily growing literacy skills (speaking, listening, reading, and writing) that make it possible for most students to actually master the content they will meet in high school and college. As Neil Postman put it, "knowledge of a subject means knowledge of the *language* of that subject....As one learns the *language* of a subject, one is also learning what the subject is" (p. 156; our italics). Ironically, it is not more, better lectures that render complex ideas accessible to eager minds; it is the growth of those minds themselves in their ability to manipulate language. In this chapter, we examine a second stage in the development of speaking and listening skills: the mastery of those skills. Here we will revisit the characteristics listed while examining strategies that experienced facilitators use to help participants—regardless of their age—toward true expertise in speaking and listening.

Seminar Partners

We said in the last chapter that early seminars tend to be dominated by a few participants, while the majority of those in the circle lapse into watchful passivity. As individuals gain more self-awareness and confidence, this domination by a few starts to wane, and a more balanced dialogue develops. Talkative and quiet participants begin to practice the skills of the other, thereby reducing the feel of a polarized event. Eventually, transferring skills from this sort of practice supports healthy relationships throughout life.

Several years ago, in an Advanced Seminar Facilitation workshop, a fifth-grade teacher (call him Kelly O'Toole) shared with us his seminar portfolio from the first semester. In that portfolio were the texts, plans, notes, and maps from the seminars he had led between August and December. He used the map from the last seminar to illustrate his concern.

Mr. O'Toole explained that during the first half of the year, his fifth graders had learned to share the discussion more equitably. Instead of only four students dominating the conversation, there were now six or seven who regularly spoke more than four times. In addition, most of his students were speaking at least once voluntarily (after the initial round-robin sequence). There were still predictable patterns, however, that bothered Mr. O'Toole: His class was made up of sixteen girls and only eight boys, and the girls tended to take almost 90 percent of the student talk time. Of those doing most of the talking, five were girls; and there were still four boys who rarely spoke voluntarily at all.

With Mr. O'Toole's permission, we made copies of his seminar map (Figure 5.1, page 34) and shared it with the entire Advanced Seminar Facilitation class. When we discussed it as a whole group, several other patterns began to emerge. Because Mr. O'Toole typically let his students choose where to sit in the discussion circle, the boys (with one exception) tended to sit together in a row, seeking social solidarity. This created a sort of "dead zone" in the seminar circle, an area that produced almost no comments. It also emerged that two of the girls who didn't talk sat together to one side of the teacher, where they were all but out of Mr. O'Toole's line of sight.

After some preliminary discussion, we used Mr. O'Toole's seminar map to illustrate a technique that we have come to call "Seminar Partners." Essentially, Seminar Partners involves using the students themselves as resources in helping the more talkative participants share the talk turns and helping the more reluctant students learn to speak up comfortably. In a situation like the one Mr. O'Toole described, we pointed out how he could reseat the participants in his class by alternating quiet and talkative, thereby creating pairs

Figure 5.1. Mr. O'Toole's Seminar Map

Mr. O'Toole

Fifth Grade

Text: _____   Date: _____

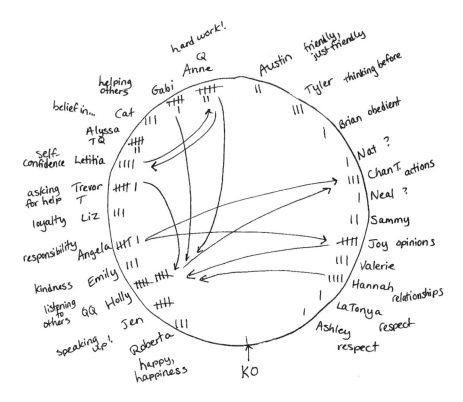

of students made up of mixed communication habits. Each pair would become "seminar partners" for a given period of time, usually a quarter or semester, and they would work together in response to a variety of reading, speaking, and listening challenges.

We also suggested that during his next seminar, he develop a plan with at least two "paired" questions that would work in a modified "pair-share" design. That is, he should have seminar partners discuss the opening question before sharing a response with the whole group, and then later ask that they follow a similar pattern with one of the core questions. He should also ask that the two participants in each pair take turns as spokesperson, thereby sharing between them at least part of the talk turns that naturally fell their way. The goal was to create a safe environment for the more reticent participants to discuss their ideas and to provide them with a structure that eased them naturally into the flow of the conversation—with their partners to help them adjust.

Mr. O'Toole worked on his proposed seating order overnight and returned to the training the next day with the following chart (Figure 5.2, page 36), which he explained in some detail, again stressing that he had taken great care to create effective teams in assigning partners.

He admitted that he had paired his worst discipline problem with a boy who was especially gifted at helping her function in a group setting. Mr. O'Toole explained, "He always speaks slowly and calmly to her and listens patiently no matter how loud she gets. Eventually, she begins to speak more respectfully, almost as if she's mimicking him. As I was reseating my students, I realized that it wasn't just about who talked and who didn't; it was also about putting all my students in a position to be successful in the seminar regardless of the nature of their challenges." When we asked the other teachers in the training to follow Mr. O'Toole's example during the second half of the school year, they all agreed that they faced similar problems and would also use Seminar Partners as one strategy for helping their seminar groups evolve.

As seminar groups of all ages become more experienced, they often learn how to focus more consistently on the person who is speaking with fewer and fewer sidebar conversations. Although this is an improvement over the distracted and distracting behavior that many participants exhibit in their first seminars, it still isn't the ideal. One way that Tracy Simmons, our experienced third-grade teacher, helps students take the next step in learning to pay attention is by asking them to focus on the content of each other's statements.

Figure 5.2. Mr. O'Toole's New Seating Order

Mr. O'Toole

Fifth Grade

Text: _____   Date: _____

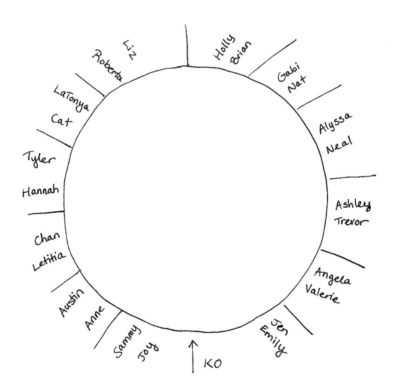

Once my students have gotten very good at "showing listening," at dramatizing what listening looks like for the sake of the person who is speaking, then I start to work on having them actually pay attention to what's being said. I tried having them repeat what the last person said before sharing their own ideas and that helped. We made big progress later in the year when I introduced "What did you learn?" as my closing question. I asked the kids to name at least one thing they learned from another participant, referring to them by name, during the course of the seminar.

Ms. Simmons freely admits that at first the answers she got in response to this question were very simplistic, but that by the end of the year, her students' responses grew in both length and complexity, in part because she continued to stress not just *what did you hear* but *what did you learn*. In this way, she helped them build a sense of coherence and expand their thinking from recall to synthesis.

Note-Taking and Reflection

Just as Ms. Simmons learned how to build on her initial commitment to teaching her third graders to pay attention to each other's ideas, the middle school social studies teacher, Marcia Cowan, also learned to push her students toward more sophisticated thinking and communication by having them take notes during the discussion.

When I first asked my students to take notes during seminar discussion, the results were mixed. Most of them would fill in the blanks on the graphic organizers that I was painstakingly creating, but only a few would actually use their notes in post-seminar writing assignments. When I discussed seminar note-taking with my colleagues, several suggested that being forced to take notes might even distract my students from really listening to the discussion. I felt like I wanted something less mechanical and more productive.

Over a holiday break, Ms. Cowan went back to the "source," as she called it—Mortimer Adler's *How to Speak How to Listen*—where she had originally read about note-taking as an aid to listening.

What she discovered is that truly skillful listening involves using your memory to reflect on what you have heard. Even though conversation is a spontaneous experience, the thinking that results can and should continue even after the conversation is over. This is certainly the case when the conversation is a more formal dialogue with the stated purpose of thinking deliberately about a complex text. One's initial thoughts while listening to the ideas of others

> *Truly skillful listening involves using your memory to reflect on what you have heard.*

are first impressions that need to be worked out over time. For this reason, memory becomes a key ingredient in the ability to listen thoughtfully. On a more practical level, this is the organic reason for note-taking. Taking notes doesn't just help you to focus on what someone else is saying; it also gives you a reference point for further reflection.

When Ms. Cowan returned to *How to Speak How to Listen*, she discovered that Adler prescribes two kinds of notes: the ones you take while listening and the ones you take upon reflection.

> The notes you take while listening record what you have done with your mind to take in what you have heard. That record enables you to go on to the second step, which I regard as equally important to the activity of listening. What you have noted during the course of listening, together with what your memory retains of what was said, provide you with food for thought.

> The thinking you then do should lead you to make a second set of notes, much more orderly, much more comprehensive, and much more critical. These concluding notes constitute the completion of the task of active listening. You have used your mind as well as possible in response to what, in the speech you heard, you thought was worthy of attention and comment. (p. 100)

"I was stunned," she admits, "by Adler's connection between listening and thinking. I had forgotten that the real purpose behind the seminar is to inspire students to think in new and creative ways, and Adler reminded me that note-taking was just a means to that particular end."

So Ms. Cowan started over. "I knew I wanted my students to do more writing post-seminar, using the discussion to inspire their thinking, so I decided to give them a writing prompt prior to the seminar itself and suggest—not require—that they might take notes along the way." She had one of her students who was a gifted artist paint Francis Bacon's epigram on the wall over her whiteboard: "Reading maketh a full man [or woman]; conference a ready man; and writing an exact man," to serve as a constant reminder to her students how speaking and listening were intimately related to writing. With each seminar, she posted either a journal or essay prompt on the whiteboard prior to the seminar itself. This time around, a hint was enough.

> Once I explained to my students that the seminar text and questions were a preview to the writing that I was going to have them do, a third of my students began taking notes voluntarily. In the next seminar, it was a half, and by the end of the semester, almost all were into it. And the beautiful thing was that Adler's second type of note-tak-

ing—rewriting your notes upon reflection—was fulfilled naturally when it came time to sketch in a journal entry or outline an essay.

What Ms. Cowan discovered was that the natural extension of discussion into writing only enhanced her student's listening skills, and that note-taking could be an organic part of the whole.

Complex Thinking and Linguistic Fluency

Just as continued and consistent dialogue practice can enhance listening skills, it is also the most organic way to develop the speaking skills that complement listening. Often, after several years of practice, the majority of students make clear and accurate statements and generally speak with the appropriate pace and volume. Even their vocabulary and grammar will improve with practice in speaking standard English. This level of proficiency, however, is only the first step. As students continue developing their thinking skills, it helps to increase their fluency. Fluency in this case doesn't just mean a larger vocabulary; it also means an increased ability to combine language (or symbols) for expressing complex thoughts clearly. An interesting example of this we've seen in recent years is a high school English teacher from Pennsylvania named Robert "Bob" Hunt, known to his students affectionately as the "Professor." After almost a decade of teaching his students to enjoy seminars, Bob Hunt became convinced that students' speaking and listening skills could more powerfully complement each other.

> Even my best students, those who could write quite naturally in compound and complex sentences, didn't use the same level of sentence structure when they spoke up in the seminar circle. One year, I audio-recorded a whole set of seminars and over the summer, as part of a course I was taking, I categorized the sentences that my students used according to whether they were simple, compound, or complex. Needless to say, the majority were simple constructions, often just sentence fragments.

Even though his reading in simple linguistics convinced him that this was natural because so much of the meaning in conversation is conveyed non-verbally, Hunt decided he wanted to find out what would happen if he taught his students to become more aware of oral and written sentence structures. He continues:

> I tried several things. First, I was honest with the kids about what our goal was, and early in the year, we had a short review on types of sentences. Then I posted examples of the more complex types on the board during seminar discussion. Then, for each seminar, I gave my students at least one of the seminar questions in advance and

had them compose a draft answer in writing in advance of the actual discussion.

"Professor" Hunt reports that these two measures worked but that they were still somewhat mechanical. In the beginning, he got more complex statements but only in response to the questions he'd handed out in advance.

> Then, I went one step further. I began to ask follow up questions during the seminar itself that required that students put two or more elements into relationship with each other. In my seminar plan, I called these "juxtaposition questions" to remind myself that I was after more complex statements in response. Rather than ask if the students agreed or disagreed with something that had just been said, I would ask: "What part of that statement do you agree with and what part do you disagree with?" Or I'd ask them how two or more elements (characters, settings, actions, even words) were related.

When he contacted us with this idea, we encouraged "Professor" Hunt to start writing his "juxtaposition" questions into all his seminar plans, typically late in the core of the discussion. He reported that his students struggled at first, but he kept on asking these types of questions, and as the year went on, his 11th graders became increasingly more analytical about written and oral grammatical structures.

But the story didn't end there. Bob Hunt found something unexpected. As his students become more comfortable with intellectual complexity, they realized how thinking (through speech and in writing) *transcends* compound and complex grammatical constructions.

He explains:

> I started out thinking that complex thoughts required complex sentences to express them. That simple expression equaled simple thinking and complex expression equaled complex thinking. What actually happened is that after struggling to articulate a complicated thought through several drafts (spoken *or* written drafts), we all finally figured out that ideally, one makes simple, clear statements to communicate complex issues.

And the result: Seminar discussions that delved much more deeply into the paradox and ambiguity of the ideas, issues, and problems at the heart of the text.

Judging a Text Fairly

Because linguistic fluency is related to fluid thought, improved speaking skills also enable students to see more clearly into the seminar text. After several years of dialogue experience, participants are typically referring to the text much more often, noting details related to sequence, category, purpose, or point of view. This increased attention to the text leads to an understanding that is both clearer and more objective, which enables the student to actually assess the value of the text as a source of insight or even truth. In *How to Read a Book*, Mortimer Adler and Charles van Doren argue that the very last stage in analytic reading is to judge the texts being read for "their truth, their clarity, or their power to enlighten" (p. 165). The ability to judge a text fairly, however, comes only after a detailed and open-minded examination—which, in turn, comes only with practice.

For an example of the kinds of speech that lead to fair and open-minded judgment, let's examine an adult seminar that took place recently. The setting was a faculty seminar in a middle school located in a large Southern city. The staff had been implementing the Paideia Seminar for a number of years, so those present that day, with few exceptions, had been involved in planning and leading seminars for a number of years.

In this particular case, the text was an excerpt from *The World Is Flat: A Brief History of the Twenty-First Century*, the bestselling book by Thomas L. Friedman that analyzes globalization at the beginning of the 21st century. The title is a metaphor for viewing the world as an economic "level playing field," where all competitors have an equal opportunity. The excerpt we used quotes Karl Marx at length and argues that economic forces are essentially creating a sort of cultural homogenization across the face of the planet, eroding the differences between the peoples of the world. The participants in the seminar found this argument so disturbing that they spent the first half of the seminar focused on a two-sentence passage:

> Some obstacles to a frictionless global market are truly sources of waste and lost opportunities. But some of these inefficiencies are institutions, habits, cultures, and traditions that people cherish precisely because they reflect nonmarket values like social cohesion, religious faith, and national pride. (p. 204)

Eventually, the seminar leader challenged them to place these sentences in context, asking repeatedly for part-to-whole thinking and what these sentences meant based on other sections of the text. As the discussion slowly widened to include other material from the excerpt, it took on more depth. Late in the discussion, the facilitator asked the participants if, indeed, they accepted Friedman's thesis that economics was "flattening" the differences between peoples. At this stage, several of those present pointed out what they believed to be fallacies in his argument, referring to assumptions he was making (e.g., that economics is the most important factor in human decision-making; that we love our possessions most of all), which, in their view, did not always hold. Eventually, the facilitator brought the discussion back around to the original concern:

Facilitator: Now, let's return to the passage that a number of you identified originally. What do you now think about its significance?

Cherise: I'm more willing to admit he's right at this point. Not right all the way, but right in that economic forces are incredibly powerful.

Will: I agree. I like the way you said that—right but not right all the way. We do have a choice in terms of what we are willing to keep despite the economic temptation to surrender our differences.

Facilitator: What kinds of things do you mean when you say "what we are willing to keep"?

Will: Things like social traditions, language, even religious differences. The things that define who we are separate from money.

Facilitator: So, in the final analysis, is what Friedman says true?

Nancy: Yes and no.

Facilitator: Yes and no?

Cherise: Perhaps the best way to say it is that his thesis is true, but in a more limited way than he seems to believe.

True but limited: That judgment was an expansion from the group's original reaction, and it was the result of almost an hour of discussion. To help the participants arrive at this juncture, the facilitator asked repeatedly that they consider the entire text before them, and to set their emotions aside in order to think together about what Friedman is actually saying. They began to explore inferences and test assumptions (their own as well as Friedman's) in a more analytical and less emotional way, so that their understanding of the text was much deeper than after the initial reading.

What this dialogue illustrates is how the practice of considering contradictions helps broaden one's frame of reference. Interestingly, a close reading of Plato's *Dialogues* reveals that Socrates himself was in the habit of analyzing real and apparent contradictions. The *Dialogues* clearly illustrate that the ability to discuss a text with an open mind supports more fluent speech and more sophisticated thought.

Identifying Multiple Perspectives

Part of the ability to discuss a complex text with an open mind involves the willingness to entertain multiple perspectives. Jacques Barzun goes directly to this point when he writes that "the starting point of conversation is contradiction" (p. 62). By this he does not mean stubborn partisanship but rather the articulation of contradictory ideas so that they can be juxtaposed in free and open discourse. For this reason, once students have developed the ability to consider a point of view different from their own while acknowledging their bias, they can then go on to develop that ability even further. The more experienced seminar participant can accomplish these tasks:

- identify the relevance of a variety of ideas
- note the positive and negative implications of different ideas
- acknowledge how a personal perspective has evolved during the conversation
- add to a previous statement by offering a more global interpretation

In other words, the ability to recognize and discuss multiple points of view should lead through practice to a more sophisticated level of awareness in which students can at once weigh and consider a variety of perspectives. Thus, we use the word *sophistication* to mean "making more complex or inclusive" as well as "to refine."

When Colonel Grant Bird, our middle school language arts teacher, had gotten his students to disagree with each other in a civil, even constructive way, he was ready to take them further in the direction of sophistication. He said:

> Because I teach eighth grade in a Paideia School, my students have had at least two years of seminar experience when they come to me in the fall of the year. My goal, then, was to get them to the point that they could articulate different points of view, so that they could compare, contrast, and even merge those points of view into something larger. A larger understanding, you might call it.

Once his eighth graders had done several seminars as a class, Colonel Bird challenged them by setting the following group process goal: "Identify multiple perspectives in response to the same question." He coached his students to say things such as "I am hearing at least two points of view being expressed here. The first is....And the second is...." He explains:

> I often used poetry or art as a way of teaching the legitimacy of multiple perspectives. When discussing poetry, I tell my students there are almost always multiple right answers, and it's our job to identify them. Once we've identified several possible answers, I can follow up with questions that ask the kids to mix and match those answers to see what they come up with.

One of the best examples of this process came when Colonel Bird assigned Emily Dickinson's poem, "I Years had been from Home."

> *I Years had been from Home*
> *And now before the Door*
> *I dared not enter, lest a Face*
> *I never saw before*
>
> *Stare stolid into mine*
> *And ask my Business there—*
> *"My Business but a Life I left*
> *Was such remaining there?"*
>
> *I leaned upon the Awe—*
> *I lingered with Before—*
> *The Second like an Ocean rolled*
> *And broke against my ear—*
>
> *I laughed a crumbling Laugh*
> *That I could fear a Door*
> *Who Consternation compassed*
> *And never winced before.*
>
> *I fitted to the Latch*
> *My Hand, with trembling care*
> *Lest back the awful Door should spring*
> *And leave me in the Floor—*
>
> *Then moved my Fingers off*
> *As cautiously as Glass*
> *And held my ears, and like a Thief*
> *Fled gasping from the House—*

As was his habit, Colonel Bird had stressed the importance of considering multiple perspectives during the discussion; therefore, he was all the more pleased when late in the seminar the following dialogue ensued:

Col. Bird: What different perspectives have we heard thus far?

[After a pause.]

Janine: I think Rashanda said it's about looking at yourself in a mirror and how scary that can be. Tony said from the beginning that it's about exactly what it says—some old lady visiting her childhood home.

Tony [interrupting]: Some old lady with bad memories.

Janine: Some old lady with bad memories. And Tiffany says it's about having to face up to something you feel guilty about.

Col. Bird: Thank you, Janine. What do the rest of you think? [Several nods of agreement.] Then how are these three interpretations of the poem related?

Frye: You mean, like what do they have in common?

Col. Bird: Sure. Start with that.

Palmer: All three readings have to do with facing up to yourself. Having to be honest with yourself when you really don't want to be.

Frye: Yeah. Yeah, that's right, but in the end of the poem, she runs away again.

Col. Bird: Who, Frye? Who runs away again?

Frye: The "speaker of the poem," like you're always saying. He or she runs away again … [he quotes the last two lines of the poem] "And held my ears, and like a Thief/Fled gasping from the House."

Palmer: Yeah. Which means that she can't face up to herself in the end. She tries, but she can't do it.

Col. Bird: Let's take this to another level: When have you been in a position like the speaker of the poem? And what did you do?

What Grant Bird has taught his students to do is to merge multiple perspectives into a larger, more inclusive statement about the text. By the end of their eighth-grade year, he was asking those same students to write essays in which they described multiple perspectives (based on what they heard during seminar discussion) and then in the summary paragraph of their essays, propose a synthesis of those perspectives.

Learning to Ask Authentic Questions

Posing genuine open-ended questions is indicative of a mind that is seeking understanding rather than promoting a pre-determined answer.

The ability to respond to this type of prompt is indicative of linguistic and intellectual maturity. There is one more characteristic of intellectual maturity that emerges as we learn to participate in collaborative, intellectual dialogue. That is the ability to pose authentic, evocative, open-ended questions in response to an ambiguous text. Posing genuine open-ended questions is indicative of a mind that is seeking understanding rather than promoting a pre-determined answer.

To see how one teacher went about coaching her students' ability to ask genuine questions, let's visit Ms. Kristin Love's biology classroom. Ms. Love is herself convinced of the power of a good question.

> Part of it is that I personally believe that in order to teach science, you have to teach the power of the Hypothesis! In order to think like a scientist, you have to think in Hypotheses. In order to understand any scientific experiment or investigation, you have to be able to identify the Hypothesis that is being tested. That's why, when I first learned to lead seminars, I thought that they were a natural form of instruction for the science classroom. Both seminar and science are all about asking and answering questions. My high school students come to me thinking that science is all about certainty; I teach them that science is really all about exploring uncertainty.

In her early seminars with students, Ms. Love was frustrated by their seeming addiction to the "one right answer," which they believed she would provide after the seminar was over. It took her at least half the year to convince the students that she really was asking open-ended questions, with multiple "right" answers, and that she expected divergent, not convergent, thinking from them. Then she had a eureka moment of her own.

> Then one day it hit me. Most of my advanced biology students, juniors and seniors, had done seminars before, if not with me then with other teachers at school, so I began with them. We read an excerpt from Newton's *Optics* multiple times, just as we had been doing for years. Then, for homework the night before the seminar, I passed out index cards to the kids and asked them to write down in plain, simple English one open-ended question about the text that they would like to hear discussed during our seminar. Then I started using some of their questions during the core section of each seminar. As time went on and we all focused on this exercise, the questions got better and better—both more open and more provocative. It became a kind of game to see who could ask the most "significant" question. And here's the best part of all, the students started asking spontaneous questions during the seminar itself—with no prompting from me. And that's when I knew we were starting to think like scientists.

Eventually, Ms. Love began having her students revise their questions during the post-seminar writing process and began posting their questions and their first draft responses along with a copy of the text on a bulletin board outside her classroom after each seminar. Before she retired from teaching,

Kristin Love became known as the Queen of Questions—a title she wore proudly.

It is important to note just how often in these examples the exercise of proficient speaking and listening skills bled over into the writing the seminar participants did after the discussion—as if all four literacy skills (reading, speaking, listening, and writing) are fundamentally related. If, as we've been arguing, thinking is the ability to explain and manipulate a text, and learning to think is the process of explaining an manipulating increasingly complex texts successfully, then it's easy to see how the students in these classrooms are learning to think. What they say and what they write are increasingly clear, coherent, and sophisticated—even as the ideas under consideration grow in complexity. Indeed, these teachers and these students are the living embodiment of the quote painted on the wall of Ms. Cowan's classroom—Francis Bacon's maxim: "Reading maketh a full man [or woman]; conference a ready man; and writing an exact man." Perhaps even more significantly, they are also the living embodiment of the lifelong effort to listen and speak more skillfully.

Chapter Five in Sum

All students have the capacity to master speaking and listening skills. These skills are both social skills (in that they enable successful social relations) and thinking skills (in that they inform and sharpen the individual's thought process).

After several years of consistent seminar experience, it is not unusual for a group of participants to exhibit individually and collectively many of the following attributes:

♦ dialogue that is more nearly balanced in terms of the talkative and the quiet participants

♦ dialogue in which more participants look at the person speaking and rarely talk while another is speaking

♦ participants yielding to another as a way of sharing talk time

♦ participants paraphrasing the comments of others

♦ participants making clear and accurate statements, using appropriate pace, volume, vocabulary, and grammar

♦ participants offering relevant and detailed comments in terms of sequence, purpose, and point of view

♦ participants referring regularly to the text or another relevant source

- participants considering another point of view while acknowledging their own bias
- participants asking authentic questions
- participants taking notes either on the text or on the comments of others

Students/participants in these types of seminars have reached what might be termed an intermediate level of skill development, and their teachers must continue to coach their speaking and listening skills in order for them to reach mastery.

6

Developing the Mind Through Dialogue

"The purpose of education is to develop a good mind. Everybody should have equal access to the kind of education most likely to develop such a mind and should have it for as long as it takes to acquire enough intellectual excellence to fix once and for all the vision of the continuous need for more and more intellectual excellence."
—Robert Maynard Hutchins

In the previous two chapters, we have shown you how experienced Paideia educators coach the development of their students' speaking and listening skills through the consistent practice of the Paideia Seminar. What we didn't say but should now acknowledge is that this requires a significant investment of time and energy on the part of the teacher as well as her or his students. Just like reading and writing, speaking and listening are complex skills that can take years to master. Teachers often worry about the time involved in teaching these skills even when they are emphasized in the standards, as they are in the Common Core State Standards.

The truth is that in teaching speaking and listening with the same intense dedication we give to reading and writing, we are also teaching thinking. In other words, as students practice these skills with increasingly complex texts, they are simultaneously learning to think about the ideas and values in those texts. They are learning to think coherently about the curriculum, and therein lies the justification for a very real investment of educational time and energy. In this chapter, we want to show very clearly how the individual mind grows in insight and understanding by participating in dialogue: in other words, how we learn to think through speaking and listening with others.

The Exercise of Conversation

More than 400 years ago, the French philosopher and essayist Michel de Montaigne wrote:

> The most fruitful and natural exercise of the mind, in my opinion, is conversation; I find the use of it more sweet than of any other action of life; and for that reason it is that, if I were now compelled to choose, I should sooner, I think, consent to lose my sight, than my hearing and speech. ("The Art of Conference," p. 446)

The first and greatest of essayists, then, calls conversation "the most fruitful and natural exercise of the mind." More than 350 years later, one of our own greatest essayists, Jacques Barzun, followed Montaigne when he wrote in *The House of Intellect* that "the finest achievement of human society and its rarest pleasure is conversation" (p. 62). If we are willing to accept their combined argument, then let us consider why conversation is at once the "most fruitful and [yet rarest] exercise of the mind." In part, it is because both Montaigne and Barzun are using the word *conversation* not to mean "casual talk" but rather something far more significant like the "free and inspired exchange of ideas." Our task is to see how conversation exercises and grows the mind more completely than any other classroom ritual.

First, let's examine how speaking and listening are intertwined in conversation. Speech is how one drafts his or her ideas during dialogue. Listening is how one internalizes the ideas of others. As with reading and writing, it is probably impossible to become quite skilled at one without also practicing the other. The only way to practice the two together is in conversation where the time spent talking is shared more-or-less equitably among those involved.

As we discussed in Chapter One, several different levels of speech occur as one's thoughts emerge. As Vygotsky and others have pointed out, first there is inner speech, which for most of us is relatively unorganized; the meaning is often not clear, even to ourselves. Then, when we do verbalize our thoughts, it is often in the form of thinking out loud, which means that often we're drafting our thoughts in spoken form, to try to understand them ourselves. This sort of tentative thinking out loud often occurs in seminar—as it should. This is the spoken equivalent of a written first draft, and while it is usually more coherent than inner speech, it probably isn't our final statement on a question. Finally, there is a more considered, more polished speech that is made with others in mind, thoughts that are now ready for public consideration. All these levels of speech go on during a seminar discussion, and the facilitator can and should encourage thinking out loud (perhaps more common early in a seminar) as well as more considered, more synthetic statements (often more prevalent later in a seminar).

Furthermore, as we listen to the emerging thoughts of others, so our own thinking should be enriched as we take multiple points of view into consideration. Our own thinking out loud is often in response to what we've heard others say or attempt to say. Our own more finished, more polished statements include the original thoughts of others as well as our own. In other words, as the seminar evolves, what one has to say can and should be enhanced by the insights of others, and vice-versa. The more voices there are in the chorus (up to a point), the richer the mix of ideas. In true conversation, these multiple ideas or perspectives merge fluidly with each other, both inside the mind of the individual and in the intellectual space shared by all those involved. The result is an intellectual whole greater than the sum of its parts.

The depth and quality of the understanding reflected in a given seminar discussion is directly related to the depth and quality of the understanding that grows up in the minds of the individuals present. The individual mind is inspired by the group, and the group is inspired by the individual mind. If those involved are skilled enough (and in the last two chapters, we have watched experienced facilitators coach the necessary skills), the result is a synthesis of multiple perspectives that is more sophisticated and explains more of the world than any one person's insight did in the beginning. This is why, when we ask a group of participants how many of them understand the text better after the seminar than before, most or all invariably raise their hands. For both the individual and the group, the movement is toward greater understanding of the ideas embedded in the text.

> *The individual mind is inspired by the group, and the group is inspired by the individual mind.*

When Montaigne writes that "the most fruitful...exercise of the mind... [is conversation]," we may take him to mean that the individual mind is exercised by the give and take of ideas, evolving in juxtaposition to each other. Montaigne goes on to describe this experience in the most vigorous terms: "If I converse with a strong mind and a rough disputant, he presses upon my flanks, and pricks me right and left; [and] his imaginations stir up mine" (p. 446).

How does the individual's perspective contribute to the group's collective understanding? To see this illustrated, let's revisit Colonel Bird's seminar on the Dickinson poem "I Years had been from Home":

Col. Bird: Can someone sum up the different perspectives we've heard thus far?

[After a pause.]

Janine: I think I can. Rashanda says it's about looking at yourself in a mirror and how scary that can be. Tony has said from the beginning that it's about exactly what it says—some old lady visiting her childhood home.

Tony [interrupting]: Some old lady with bad memories.

Janine: Some old lady with bad memories. And Tiffany says it's about having to face up to something you feel guilty about.

Col. Bird: Thank you, Janine. Does that sound right to the rest of you? [General nods of agreement.] Then can you see any ways in which these three readings of the poem could be related?

We're listening to Colonel Bird focus the group's attention on the multiple perspectives that have been expressed to that point in the seminar so that he can then ask for more synthetic thinking from his students. Eventually, the insight that all three points of view have to do with being "honest with yourself when you really don't want to be" leads to the students talking and writing about their own efforts to be honest with themselves when confronted by uncomfortable topics. Rashanda's, Tony's, and Tiffany's original thoughts about the poem have all contributed to the group's new understanding, as summarized by Palmer. Often this process happens quite naturally (recalling Montaigne's "most…*natural* exercise of the mind"); sometimes, however, the facilitator must deliberately draw attention to it as Colonel Bird does here. Experienced seminar participants often provide much the same sort of group meta-cognition by voluntarily juxtaposing different perspectives or asking others to do so. The idea, whether the facilitator or participant raises the point, is to highlight how individual insights can be synthesized in collective understanding.

It is worth noting at this point that good seminar plans feature a series of questions designed to be asked in a particular pattern (see a detailed discussion in Appendix B). They are deliberately open-ended in order to generate a wide variety of responses, thereby creating the need for a more sophisticated view of the text. In addition, the questions are of three types—opening, core, and closing—which give shape to the seminar discussion by first inviting participants into a detailed examination of the text and then inviting them to construct new understanding out of that examination. Experienced seminar facilitators not only learn how to create these question sequences on paper but also how to ask spontaneous follow-up questions during the discussion in order to nurture growth in understanding. When we train teachers to lead Paideia Seminars, our focus is on both effective planning *and* facilitation— writing good questions and revising them on the spot as necessary.

During the discussion, then, individual thoughts should feed the collective understanding. The converse is also true. The varying perspectives articulated by the members of the seminar circle feed the individual mind. To draw on the same example, Colonel Bird's student Tony began the seminar by arguing that Dickinson's poem was about "some old lady with bad memories" revisiting her childhood home. By the end of the seminar, he was speaking in terms of guilt, honesty, and self-knowledge. His original reading was quite literal; his later understanding was more sophisticated. Not only does his understanding take in the insights of his classmates; it also explains much more of the text and much more of his own experience of the world. Robert Grudin (in his superb 1996 book *On Dialogue*) calls this heightened awareness of multiple perspectives the "dialogic mind." The multiplicity of ideas expressed by the group has been internalized by the individual, who must try to make sense of them. Grudin describes what happens:

> Awareness of inner multiplicity becomes a special form of self-awareness. This self-seeing is itself a dialogic process in which the mind momentarily surrenders its pretension to coherence in an effort to understand and refine its responses. (p. 5)

What Tony's classmate Janine verbalizes in our example is the "inner multiplicity" that she has internalized from the seminar discussion. What Palmer then articulates is one effort to "understand and refine" a response to this multiplicity. In each case, we can glimpse an individual mind engaged in the dialogic process of wrestling with a multiplicity of ideas, and to craft from that process a coherent response that does justice to various ideas that have been expressed. We are listening to individual minds enriched by the group's multiple insights. As a high school student once remarked to us during post-seminar debriefing, "eventually what you learn to do is think like a seminar."

It is important to note that learning to "think like a seminar" does not mean accepting all points of view without exercising some judgment. Jacques Barzun makes this point emphatically in *The House of Intellect* when he demands that we define conversation not "as the *exchange*, but as the *sifting* of opinion" (p. 60, emphasis Barzun's).

> The genuine exercise or true conversation sifts opinion, that is, tries to develop tenable positions by alternate statements, objections, modifications, examples, arguments, distinctions, expressed with the aid of the rhetorical arts. (p. 61)

In other words, as various perspectives (or "opinions") come into play, the individual seminar participant must simultaneously keep an open mind in order to hear these opinions clearly and use his or her judgment to weigh their relative value. In this way, the various perspectives take on their proper weight in relation to each other as the individual mind merges them into something larger and more inclusive.

Sophistication and Amplitude

One way to describe what happens to the individual mind during the course of an inspiring seminar discussion is that it moves from a condition of simplicity to one of sophistication. This process is both critical—as one chooses to accept, reject, or revise new insights—and creative—as one fuses these multiple insights into a new and coherent position of one's own. This is the mind being *exercised*, to borrow Montaigne's term, and growing stronger and more flexible as a result. By practicing, we can grow our capacity to see different points of view in response to a cluster of questions.

Robert Grudin uses the word *amplitude* to describe the mind's willingness and capacity to grow when stimulated by new ideas.

> "Amplitude" connotes the desire to see a given topic *from every possible perspective*; it also connotes curiosity about and compassion for the minds of other people and other ages. (p. 6, emphasis Grudin's)

Mental flexibility (or amplitude) is something that we typically think of as characteristic of children rather than adults. More than 400 years ago, Francis Bacon, in writing "Of Custom," put it this way:

> So we see, in languages, the tongue is more pliant to all expressions and sounds, the joints are more supple, to all feats of activity and motions, in youth than afterwards. For it is true, that late learners cannot so well take the ply; except it be in some minds, that have not suffered themselves to fix, but have kept themselves open, and prepared to receive continual amendment, which is exceeding rare. (pp. 166–67)

This may be the first use of the word *open* in just this way: to describe a mind that is "prepared to receive continual amendment." Learning, especially learning that continues throughout life, is dependent on open-mindedness. Seminar dialogue, whether practiced formally in school or more informally without, is designed to inspire and reward open-mindedness—and to help us maintain an open mind even into adulthood. In our own highly complex and volatile age, it is also preparation for life, in the sense that a mind exercised by dialogue remains not just more open but also "more supple" and more creative. It retains the capacity to receive and respond to new ideas.

The ability to "receive continual amendment" from the perspectives of others requires not just an open mind; it also requires the willingness to experience the disorientation that can result when your ideas or values are threatened by those new perspectives. Grudin describes this willing suspension of certainty as that moment in "a dialogic process in which the mind momentarily surrenders its pretension to coherence" (p. 5). Many of us are unwilling to surrender our "pretension to coherence," especially when it comes to those values which we hold most dear. It was for this reason that John Stuart Mill, in *On Liberty*, counseled deliberate open-mindedness "when we turn to subjects infinitely more complicated, to morals, religion, politics, social relations, and the business of life" (p. 284). Perhaps the key to retaining our flexibility, even when discussing "morals, religion, politics, [and] social relations," is to remember that the intellectual disequilibrium that results from a flood of new perspectives is only temporary. The goal is for the individual mind to construct a new understanding that is both more inclusive (in that it explains more of the text and of the world) and more sophisticated (in that it is more subtle and more flexible). In other words, we can chart what can and should happen to an individual mind during the course of a seminar like this:

Simple Equilibrium > Disequilibrium > Sophisticated Equilibrium

Adler calls this simply the movement from "a state of understanding less to a state of understanding more." That movement, however, requires a willingness to experience the temporary state of disequilibrium in order to move through it to a greater understanding.

To illustrate what happens when seminar participants are unwilling to surrender their original positions (the state of simple equilibrium), let's examine a recent adult seminar. The setting is a seminar training institute for history teachers; we opened the institute with a model Paideia Seminar on an excerpt from the second chapter of John Stuart Mill's *On Liberty*. In this excerpt, Mill argues that:

> He who knows only his own side of the case, knows little of that. His reasons may be good, and no one may have been able to refute them. But if he is equally unable to refute the reasons on the opposite side; if he does not so much as know what they are, he has no ground for preferring either opinion. (p. 284)

As one might imagine, the seminar was intended to explore the value in examining multiple perspectives in the search for truth. Unfortunately, several participants took the discussion almost immediately to the realm of contemporary politics. Two of the most vehement represented what they were glad to label "the" conservative and "the" liberal points of view. Ironically, neither was the least interested in hearing what the other had to say but only in ridiculing the opposing perspective—first in more veiled terms, but under the pressure of opposition, in increasingly warm and personal remarks. The facilitator (one of us) struggled mightily to rein in the disagreement for several reasons: One, so that other participants might feel that it was safe to join in;

two, so that the participants might return to the text to see what Mill had to say; and three, to illustrate what can happen when people choose to listen to each other, even about a volatile topic. Eventually (after about twenty minutes of the facilitator referring the participants back to the text, the text, text!), several other participants joined the fray but in a more reasoned way. They pointed out that politics was one of the topics Mill was warning us about, and took us deeper into his argument: One earned the right to an opinion only by examining all sides of an issue. Eventually, an older teacher and coach offered this insight:

> You know, I should first confess that I have always thought of myself as a "conservative." I believe in traditional values, and I enjoyed hearing my colleague across the way [gesturing to one of the original combatants] giving our liberal friends hell. But I have to say that I think Mill is right. If we are really interested in the truth—not just winning an argument—then we have to examine all sides of an issue. I find this all the time with my students. I used to tell them that my way was the only way, but in the past few years, I've paid more attention to what they have to say, and I have to confess, they've taught me a lot. I've had to change "my way" more than once because they've convinced me what they have to say might be right. My mother used to say that listening is how you learn, and it's amazing to me that I managed to forget that for thirty years or so.

This man, along with several others, saved the seminar that day, in the sense that he revived the possibility of dialogue by giving the participants permission to be open-minded again. The original dispute had shut down the willingness on the part of most participants to speak or listen freely, and it took something like this from a participant (the facilitator wasn't enough in this case) to reopen the flow of communication.

How are we to describe the kind of thought that results when people are willing to listen? To suspend the need for certainty and experience the intellectual disorientation that comes when they listen with an open mind to new ideas? As they struggle toward a new and more sophisticated equilibrium or understanding?

As we said at the beginning of this book, learning to think is the process of explaining and manipulating increasingly complex texts successfully. By definition, increasingly complex texts contain larger numbers of discrete elements and more complex relationships between and among those elements. In other words, more complex texts explain more of the world: imagine all of *Hamlet* as opposed to one soliloquy, or the Periodic Table of the Elements as opposed to the model of a single molecule. Here, then, is the crux of the issue: Learning to think means developing the ability over time to construct more sophisticated and more successful explanations—first of texts (which are pictures of the world around us) and later of the world itself. These more sophisticated explanations account for multiple points of view and are more complex in that they explain more rather than less of human experience. For most of us, the ability to think in more sophisticated patterns takes time and practice in conversation, "the most fruitful and natural exercise of the mind."

If we break down the experience of true dialogic conversation, what do we discover? What sorts of experiences should we give ourselves and others as we proceed through life? In order to grow through rigorous conversational exercise, the individual mind must have two experiences. The first experience is the growing fluency that comes only with steady practice in speaking and listening. Each of these fundamental literacy skills represents practice in an aspect of thinking; practiced together, in conversation, they are thinking in sum. The second experience necessary for the growth of the mind is the steady exposure to a variety of other minds at work. Minds can grow only in relation to other minds in a language-rich environment.

The remarkable thing about the seminar is that it quite naturally provides both types of experience in abundance. For that reason, it provides "the most fruitful and natural exercise of the mind." Next, let us examine how to assess the quality of that intellectual exercise when it is practiced deliberately.

Chapter Six in Sum

♦ The individual mind grows in insight and understanding by participating in dialogue, and we learn how to think through speaking and listening with others.

♦ The depth and quality of the understanding reflected in any seminar discussion is directly related to the depth and quality of the understanding that grows up in the minds of the individuals present, and vice-versa.

♦ During a successful seminar discussion, the individual mind evolves from a state of simple mental equilibrium through disequilibrium to a state of more sophisticated mental equilibrium.

♦ Learning to think means developing the ability over time to construct more sophisticated and more successful explanations—first, of texts under discussion, and later, of the world itself.

♦ Ultimately, learning to speak and listen well—just like learning to think clearly and coherently—is a lifelong endeavor.

7

Assessing the Quality of Thoughtful Dialogue

*"Not everything that counts can be counted; and
not everything that can be counted counts."*
—Albert Einstein

Usually when we talk about assessing the skills of dialogue, educators immediately jump to the idea of "giving a grade." Like Kristin Love's struggle with her students' desire for "the one right answer," teachers also battle an addiction to grades—fueled in part by students, parents, and administrators. Indeed, giving a grade for a seminar can help motivate desired behavior and justify the use of class time. Given that reality, in this chapter we'll describe ways to arrive at a fair measure of a student's participation in thoughtful discussion. However, we want to be very deliberate in our use of sound measurement practices, both for the sake of giving an accurate grade and for upholding our fundamental values about the learning process. The truth is that our real purpose for assessing participants' skills is not to further manipulate, evaluate, or justify, but to give helpful feedback that will support students' growth over time.

An individual participant contributes to thoughtful dialogue not only by speaking, but also by listening and thinking. Although speaking is fairly simple to track, measuring listening and thinking skills is much more complicated. It bears repeating that speaking, listening, and thinking are *all* important habits we practice in dialogue. Therefore, all are skills that need to be coached and assessed.

Given that full participation in thoughtful dialogue includes these three interrelated skills (speaking, listening, and thinking) we use a multi-step assessment process that coincides with the Paideia Seminar cycle (Figure 7.1).

Figure 7.1. Key Steps for Assessment Within the Paideia Seminar

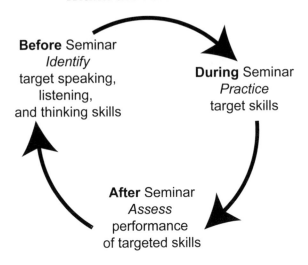

Before Seminar
Identify
target speaking,
listening,
and thinking skills

During Seminar
Practice
target skills

After Seminar
Assess
performance
of targeted skills

Setting Goals

Before any group starts a seminar, be it their first formal experience or after years of practice, we advocate taking some time to set personal and group participation goals. At this point, the more specific the goal related to speaking, listening, and thinking, the more likely one can achieve it. Often we hear teachers say they want students to "be respectful" during a seminar and certainly we agree with that idea. But what does being respectful look or sound like? It is vital to describe participation goals in clear behavioral terms that students understand. In that way, we clarify what the sub-skills of collaborative and intellectual dialogue look and sound like—both to help improve the quality of the discussion and to enable sound measurement practices. Then, we have students practice the discrete sub-skills through discussion. Finally, we assess how the students perform based on valid and reliable data.

In designing units or modules of study for the Common Core State Standards, we developed a Speaking and Listening Rubric for students and their teachers to use in collaboration (Figure 7.2). In creating and testing this rubric, we described these skills in concrete terms for clarity's sake.

Figure 7.2. Paideia Seminar Speaking and Listening Rubric

Demands and Qualities	Not Yet
Attention Engagement Articulation Explanation (Justification) Expansion Connection	♦ does not look at the person speaking ♦ occasionally turns and talks to person sitting nearby while another person is speaking ♦ does not take notes related to the ideas being discussed ♦ makes barely audible statements ♦ makes simple, somewhat unrelated or repetitive points/statements ♦ draws conclusions based on a single perspective ♦ does not ask questions ♦ does not refer to what else has been said
Demands and Qualities	**Proficient**
Attention Engagement Articulation Explanation (Justification) Expansion Connection	♦ looks at the person speaking during most of the discussion ♦ rarely talks while another is speaking ♦ occasionally takes notes related to the ideas being discussed ♦ gives way to another as a way of sharing the talk time ♦ makes clear and accurate statements; generally speaks at appropriate pace and volume ♦ uses relevant vocabulary and grammar ♦ provides points/statements about the discussion topic, noting details related to sequence, category, purpose, or point of view ♦ refers to the text or another relevant source ♦ considers another point of view and states personal bias ♦ asks authentic questions ♦ paraphrases what else has been said

Demands and Qualities	Advanced
Attention Engagement Articulation Explanation (Justification) Expansion Connection	◆ looks at the person speaking during the discussion ◆ does not talk while another is speaking ◆ consistently takes notes related to the ideas being discussed ◆ gives way to another as a way of sharing the talk time ◆ makes clear and accurate statements ◆ consistently speaks at appropriate pace and volume; uses relevant vocabulary and grammar ◆ provides insight related to fallacies within the text ◆ tests assumptions and explores inferences ◆ refers to the text or another relevant source ◆ illuminates relevance ◆ notes positive/negative implications ◆ acknowledges difference in own perspectives—before and now ◆ adds to previous statement by offering a more global/holistic interpretation ◆ refers to another facet of an idea or another's comment ◆ considers multiple points of view while acknowledging personal bias ◆ asks authentic, thought-provoking, open-ended questions

Given these steps for assessment within the Paideia Seminar cycle, the following lists contain suggested seminar process goals for students.

Representative goals for speaking:

- ◆ Speak loudly enough so that everyone can hear.
- ◆ Speak voluntarily _x_ times.
- ◆ Make clear and accurate statements.
- ◆ Use appropriate grammar and vocabulary.
- ◆ Use relevant vocabulary.
- ◆ Use a collaborative tone.

◆ Disagree agreeably or in a neutral tone.

Representative goals for listening:

◆ Look at the person speaking.

◆ Paraphrase what you hear someone say.

◆ Respond to what someone else says.

◆ Ask a question.

◆ Wait your turn to talk. (Don't talk while another is speaking.)

◆ Give way. (Be quiet if you begin talking at the same time some-one else does.)

Setting goals for thinking is more complex, which is why we use our simple definition (to explain and manipulate variables in a text) to help maintain a useful focus. We consider thinking skills as having to do with the following:

explanation/justification—to say something about the topic; to give reason(s) for what one says

expansion—moving beyond essential points and/or an assumed perspective

connection—working to bridge ideas and construct common understanding

When we break down these three categories, we can suggest these more specific, discrete thinking goals.

Representative goals for thinking:

◆ Provide insight related to fallacies within the text.

◆ Test assumptions.

◆ Explore inferences.

◆ Refer to the text or another relevant source.

◆ Illuminate relevance.

◆ Note positive/negative implications.

◆ Acknowledge difference in one's own perspective—past and present.

◆ Add to previous statement by offering a more global/holistic interpretation.

◆ Refer to another facet of an idea.

◆ Consider multiple points of view without stating a bias.

♦ Ask authentic, open-ended questions.

The ability to disagree agreeably is a speaking skill as well as a thinking skill. This is an important reminder to students that thinking together through dialogue is not a debate, but rather an investigation of ideas. The goal is to engage in thinking together about ideas in a way that leaves personal prejudices behind.

Collecting and Measuring Data

So far we have said that measurement of dialogue skills begins with clear observable goals. From there it is a matter of collecting data before, during, and after the seminar. Now let us consider how students and teachers generate solid measurement data within the various stages of the Paideia Seminar cycle.

Pre-Seminar Content

Students produce good measurement data during the very first step of the seminar cycle. Using Adler's *How to Read a Book*, students may be required to mark the text for specific features connected to the key ideas. The marked text then becomes a data source for a teacher to record. In addition, students may take notes on a graphic organizer while doing an analytical reading of the text. These notes are valuable to the student during the post-seminar writing process and equally valuable to the teacher as assessment data.

Pre-Seminar Process

For pre-seminar process, teachers often use name tents and have students write their participation goal on them (posting a list of suggestions on a board for all to see and choose from). The same can be accomplished by distributing a checklist or rubric for participation. The facilitator asks individuals to take time and reflect (perhaps looking at past data) to determine their goals for a given seminar. Committing to a personal participation goal in writing generates formative assessment data that will be used after the seminar.

Seminar Discussion

During the seminar dialogue, the facilitator takes notes or maps the discussion. The note-taking or mapping is designed to capture talk turns and key ideas. A facilitator map may also capture data specific to a given text or group of participants.

Post-Seminar Process

After the seminar dialogue, participants reflect on their target goal and assess their own participation. This is noted on whatever document (name tent, checklist, journal) they used pre-seminar to record their goals.

Post-Seminar Content

Finally, participants engage in a post-seminar content exercise that requires writing, drawing, or constructing a more concrete response. This final product has an associated rubric that students can use to refine their work and teachers can use to assess it.

The entire process, then, produces three important sets of data: a student-produced participation document (pre- and post-process), a teacher-produced seminar map (from the discussion itself), and student-produced writing (or other product) created during the pre- and post-seminar content exercises (see Figure 7.3 below).

Figure 7.3. Data Sets Created During the Seminar Cycle

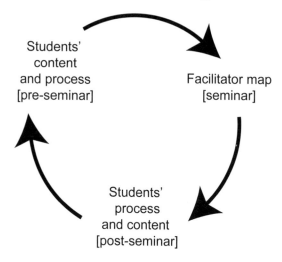

Students'
content
and process
[pre-seminar]

Facilitator map
[seminar]

Students'
process
and content
[post-seminar]

After grappling with these issues for many years, we now recommend that teachers consider the following weighted proportions.

Weighting Recommendation for Artifacts Used in Assessing Seminar:

student *process* artifacts= 45 percent

student *content* artifacts= 45 percent

teacher map= 10 percent

We believe that weighing the data sets in this way most accurately values the interrelated skills practiced during the course of an entire seminar cycle. These proportions illustrate an emphasis on reading and writing about the course content. Of equal weight is the students' self- assessment of their evolving communication skills. Finally, the teacher map is used as the leverage point as needed.

Teacher Lesson Plans and Student Samples

Following are two examples of the seminar assessment process with illustrative teacher and student seminar artifacts.

Example 1: "If It Was My Home" Seminar and Argumentative Essay

The first seminar is entitled "If It Was My Home." The electronic text and map used can be viewed at www.ifitwasmyhome.com. The teacher displayed the map of the Gulf oil spill, through a projector, onto a large screen so that all the students could see it. The teacher's lesson plan is shown on the following pages.

Pre-Seminar

Content:

—Whole class discussion about the Gulf oil spill of 2010 with questions focused on the individual's role in society; specifically, the individual's responsibility during a disaster.

—Students view the map.

Process:

Teacher leads discussion of seminar definition, roles, and responsibilities, and then has students complete the following form.

Seminar Process Assessment

Name: _____

Date: _____

Seminar Title: _____

Ideas/Values: _____

My goal for today's seminar is to (check one):

_____   Yield to another in order to share talk time

_____   Refer to the text in detail

_____   Consider multiple points of view

_____   Speak out of uncertainty

Seminar Questions

Opening Question:

What is the single most important feature on this map? (round-robin response) Why? (spontaneous discussion)

Core Questions:

(The electronic map feature is used to move oil spill into location over the student's school.)

Given this overlay map of the oil spill in our own area, what is the farthest city that the disaster will affect? How many miles away is that?

How many states are affected by the spill, and to what extent?

What would have happened if the disaster had occurred here (Colorado, Tennessee, North Carolina)?

How would our elevation affect the outcome of the oil spill?

How would another type of manmade disaster affect our lives (nuclear reactor meltdown)? Why?

Closing Questions:

What do you think is an individual's responsibility during a disaster like this? What can you do as an individual?

Post-Seminar

Process:

Students complete the following self-assessment prompt.

On a scale of one to five (one being not so good and five being excellent), I would rate myself as a _____ in relationship to my seminar goal because…

Writing Prompt:

What is the proper role of the individual in response to a disaster? After reading various perspectives on individual responsibility and examining an interactive map of the 2010 Gulf oil disaster, write a letter to a younger child that describes the disaster and argues for the proper individual response. Support your position with evidence from the texts. Be sure to examine competing views. Give examples from past or current events to illustrate your position.

Sixth-grade students will be writing letters to an unnamed second- or third-grade student. These letters will be delivered to a primary grades classroom in the same (or a sister) school, and the younger students will be invited to respond.

Even though this piece of writing is in the form of a letter addressed to an individual, the form will remain that of a formal essay, so that the teacher can coach essay and paragraph construction, as well as sentence structure and content.

The teacher can use the following rubric to score the student essays (developed by the Common Core State Standards Literacy Design Collaborative):

LDC Argumentation Classroom Assessment Rubric	
MEETS EXPECTATIONS	
Focus	Addresses the prompt and stays on task; provides a generally convincing response.
Reading/Research	Demonstrates generally effective use of reading material to develop an argument.

Controlling Idea	Establishes a credible claim and supports an argument that is logical and generally convincing. (L2) Acknowledges competing arguments while defending the claim.
Development	Develops reasoning to support claim; provides evidence from text(s) in the form of examples or explanations relevant to the argument. (L3) Makes a relevant connection(s) that supports argument.
Organization	Applies an appropriate text structure that develops reasons.
Conventions	Demonstrates a command of standard English conventions and cohesion; employs language and tone appropriate to audience and purpose.
NOT YET	
Focus	Attempts to address prompt but lacks focus or is off-task.
Reading/Research	Demonstrates weak use of reading material to develop argument.
Controlling Idea	Establishes a claim and attempts to support an argument but is not convincing. (L2) Attempts to acknowledge competing arguments.
Development	Reasoning is not clear; examples or explanations are weak or irrelevant. (L3) Connection is weak or not relevant.
Organization	Provides a weak text structure; composition is confusing.
Conventions	Demonstrates a weak command of standard English conventions; lacks cohesion; language and tone are not appropriate to audience and purpose.

On the next pages, you'll see sample post-seminar work from two students, James and Micha.

Seminar Process Assessment

The Individual and the Community

Name: _James_

Date: _8/24/10_

Seminar Title: _If It Was My Home_

Ideas/Values: _responsibility, community_

My goal for today's seminar is to (check one):

√	Yield to another in order to share talk time
___	Refer to the text in detail
___	Consider multiple points of view
___	Speak out of uncertainty

On a scale of one to five (one being not so good and five being excellent), I would rate myself as a _2_ in a relationship to my seminar goal. Because _I really didn't talk as much so I couldn't have completed my goal._

James's Essay

(Note that the student's errors have
been retained for authenticity.)

Dear Friend,

Hey I hope your year has been great. I remember the trip to Jekyl Island, and I hope you are going to like it. We are working on a question in Mrs. Freeman's class. It is do you have a responsibility to respond when others are affected by a disaster? You think it is so easy right well, it isn't that easy.

I am going to be citing quotes from Dalai Lama and an 11 year old girl named Olivia Bouler. They are going to help you understand, and maybe change your mind. I used to think that I don't need to help others, but now I think after reading about these other people I think that you should try and help others no matter what race or if they are a family member or not because they are apart of the same world.

First, Dalai Lama "I try to treat whoever I meet as an old friend." This compares to my thesis because when you go somewhere you should try to treat them like you have been their friend for a long time. Don't be afraid to ask questions about how their day has been going.

Another, Dalai Lama is "Because we all share an identical need for love." I chose this because it supports what I'm trying to tell you in my thesis. It should be understandable because you can tell the attempt to try and make the reader understand people need love.

Finally, Olivia Bouler "I believe that one person can make a difference. I chose this because one person can make a difference in this world." You can be the only one helping a cause, but you will make a difference and help what cause you're trying to help.

Now you understand why these author changed my mind. It would be great if you try to change the world. There are lots of hurricanes, tornadoes, earthquakes, etc. that happen in this world Like what Olivia Bouler said, "One person can make a difference." This world is full of different faces. So, I'm asking you to help other people in this world.

Sincerely,

James, 6th grader

Seminar Process Assessment

The Individual and the Community

Name: Micha

Date: 8/24/10

Seminar Title: If It Was My Home

Ideas/Values: _____

My goal for today's seminar is to (check one):

√   Yield to another in order to share talk time

_____   Refer to the text in detail

_____   Consider multiple points of view

_____   Speak out of uncertainty

On a scale of one to five (one being not so good and five being excellent), I would rate myself as a 4 1/2 in a relationship to my seminar goal. Because I gave myself a 4 because I did really good but still talked a lot. Also because I would try to let others talk but they told me to go.

Micha's Essay

Dear Friend,

I remember when I was in kindergarten. I had so much fun making gingerbread houses and finding the gingerbread man. I also remember phase-in where we tried out all the stations and made cookie cats with candy faces and we learned about seminar by studying famous paintings. But now, in 6th grade, we had a seminar on this question; do you have a responsibility to respond when others are affected by disaster? Before the seminar I thought maybe just a little about others, but after the seminar I thought, "Sure, I am responsible because we all live in the same world." To help us understand, our teacher gave us some texts that also helped us and we discussed the recent oil spill and if we have any responsibilities in this disaster.

In our text called "Traveling through the Dark," I chose to talk about three statements. The first is "I thought hard for us all." The man in the story had to choose to save the life of a baby deer or save the lives of people who could be hurt if he didn't move it out of the road. I chose that statement because in my mind I had a decision to make. I think I made the best decision. I chose not to just care about me and my family and friends but to care about everyone. I really like the part, "for us all" because it's not just talking about helping him but helping everyone. That is how it relates to my thesis (idea)!

The second statement is, "It is usually best." I chose that because it is usually best to care about everyone. It was best for the people to move the deer, but it was not best for the deer. Even though you could help someone you know you can also help people you don't know. He did the right thing by pushing the deer out of the way. I would have done that, too.

The last statement I chose was, "I hesitated." This phrase fits my thesis. I think that because in the middle of my thesis I hesitated. Not literally, but my actions. For example, when the teacher showed the oil spill as if it happened in Chattanooga, I changed my thoughts. Like in the story, he hesitated about what to do before he pushed the deer out of the road.

We have been including the oil spill in a lot of papers we have written. Now that I know more about it, I have changed my mind and think that we should care about everyone no matter where they are. John Donne said, "Every man is a piece of the continent." You should be a part of the world. You are the only person that can decide which side you will choose. You can help the world like I want do, or you can be in a bubble and just watch. Make a change in this world.

Your Friend,

Micha

"If It Was My Home" Seminar Map

Sixth Grade

Text: "If It Was My Home"   Date: 8/24/10

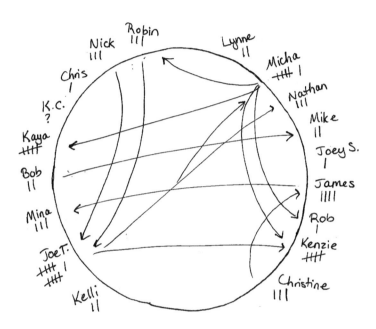

Grades for "If It Was My Home" Seminar

James:

       Pre-content: B

       Process: B

       Post-content: C

       Map: talked a good amount, cited text

       Overall grade for seminar: B-

Micha:

       Pre-content: B

       Process: B

       Post-content: A

       Map: talked a good amount, cited text

       Overall grade for seminar: A-

Example 2: "Cupid and Psyche" Seminar and Personal Narrative Essay

The second seminar is entitled "Cupid and Psyche." The teacher's lesson plan reads as follows.

Pre-Seminar

Content:

—Class discussion of a myth. A *myth* is something that illustrates the world view of a people (not as something imaginary, unfounded, or false). The teacher asks questions that help students see a connection with the theme of personal change.

—Students do an Inspectional read, numbering the paragraphs and noting definitions for unfamiliar vocabulary within text.

—Students do an Analytical read, marking text to note instances of personal decisions and change, i.e. "D."

Process:

—Teacher leads discussion of seminar definition, roles and responsibilities, and then has students complete the Seminar Process Assessment, as shown on page 82.

Seminar Questions

Opening Question:

What is this story designed to teach? (After everyone responds, allow for spontaneous explanations. Encourage participants to cite the text.)

Core Questions:

How does jealousy motivate action in this myth?

Why does Cupid conceal his identity from Psyche after she loves him?

How is Psyche transformed?

In Greek, the word *psyche* means both "butterfly" and "soul." How do these definitions contribute to the allegory?

Closing Question:

Psyche makes some bad choices but is changed by her experiences. What changes have you chosen to make?

Post-Seminar

Process:

Students complete self-assessment prompt (as shown on page 82).

Writing Prompt:

How does change affect those involved in the process? After reading the myth "Cupid and Psyche" and thinking about the nature of change, write a personal narrative that relates an important moment of change in your own life. Use strong, purposeful, sensory details to deepen the experience of your reader and to further develop your work.

In scoring these student narratives, the teacher can use the following Personal Narrative rubric.

Personal Narrative Writing Rubric

	You're There! 93–100	Pretty close. 85–92	Somewhat. 75–84	Not yet. 60–74
Personal Narrative Content				
Small Moment	The narrative is a very detailed description of a small moment that includes only enough additional information to help the narrative make sense.	The narrative is mostly a small moment, but there are a few details that don't support the moment and could be removed.	The narrative includes a small moment and lots of other details, or may include several small moments, rather than one.	The narrative has no clear small moment around which it is built.

Rubric continues on next page.

	You're There! 93–100	Pretty close. 85–92	Somewhat. 75–84	Not yet. 60–74
Sensory Details	The narrative is filled with rich, sensory details that bring the writing alive.	The narrative has a few sensory details that add some interest.	The narrative has a couple of sensory details that don't add much to the narrative for the reader.	The author didn't use sensory details at all to add richness to the text.
Moment of Change	The personal narrative describes an important moment of change for the author.	The author mentions the change, but doesn't describe it clearly. Also, the moment may be mentioned but not described.	The author mentions the change that took place, but doesn't describe it at all.	The author doesn't include the change or lesson information.
Expected Writing Skills				
Comma focus: items in series, two adjectives with noun, and compound sentence	Commas are used correctly in almost every situation.	Commas are mostly used correctly. There may be two or three times where you have misplaced a comma.	Commas are misplaced several times.	Comma usage doesn't follow any of the rules discussed in class. This seriously interferes with your meaning.
I and *Me*	*I* and *me* are used correctly.	*I* and *me* are used incorrectly once or twice.	*I* and *me* are used incorrectly between three and five times.	*I* and *me* are frequently used incorrectly.
Subjects and Predicates	Subjects and predicates agree in number.	There are a couple of subject and predicate errors, but the meaning is mostly clear.	There are several errors in agreement and your meaning is lost at times.	There are so many errors in agreement that your meaning is quite impossible to follow.

	You're There! 93–100	Pretty close. 85–92	Somewhat. 75–84	Not yet. 60–74
Spelling	Spelling is almost perfect.	There are a few spelling errors, but no meaning is lost.	There are quite a few spelling errors and your meaning is at times unclear.	There are so many spelling errors your work is really difficult to read and understand.
Overall Readability	Your narrative is clearly written, your sentences are well written, and the details work together to tell your story.	Your narrative is mostly clear, your sentences may have a few errors in them, and your details are mostly clear.	Your narrative is flawed to the point that it is difficult to follow, you may have several errors, and your details don't work to support your story.	Your narrative is very flawed to the point it is difficult to understand. Also, your details are random and offer no support for your story.

Seminar Process Assessment

The Outcome of Change

Name: _James_

Date: _12/2/10_

Seminar Title: _Cupid and Psyche_

Ideas/Values: _Change, Metamorphosis, Decisions_

My goals for today's seminar are to (check two):

√	Yield to another in order to share talk time
√	Refer to the text in detail
___	Consider multiple points of view
___	Speak out of uncertainty

On a scale of one to five (one being not so good and five being excellent), I would rate myself as a _4 1/2_ in a relationship to my seminar goal. Because _I referred to the text mostly but I didn't yield to others that much._

James's Inspectional and Analytical Read

Mark decisions/ choices made by character(s) with a "D."

James

Cupid and Psyche

(Prep-"D"s arent specific.)
88

better than

1.) Once upon a time there was a king with three daughters, all were lovely, but the youngest named Psyche, excelled her sisters in beauty so much that she seemed like a goddess. The fame of her beauty spread far and wide and soon many people came to worship her. Meanwhile the real goddess of love, Venus (Aphrodite) became neglected as fewer people came to her temples to make offerings and pay her homage. *not cared for*

D   gifts   respect/honor

2.) Venus grew jealous of Psyche and turned to her son Cupid (Eros) for help. She told Cupid to *disgusting* go and shoot Psyche with an arrow as to make her fall in love with the most vile and horrible creature on the earth. Cupid took up his bow and arrow, flew earthward, had one look at Psyche and was lost. No victim of his gold arrows was more deeply in love than he.

feelings

3.) While everyone worshipped and admired Psyche, her beauty was so awesome that men were fearful to express their longing and desire for her or make plain their sentiments. Both her sisters though less lovely than Psyche had gotten married. So Psyche sat sad and solitary, only to be admired but not loved. *alone*

fortuneteller

4.) Psyche's father began to suspect some curse had fallen on his youngest daughter, and went to the nearby town of Miletus to consult the oracle of Apollo. The oracle said that Psyche was to be dressed in clothes of mourning and placed on the summit of a mountain. There she would be *grieving* taken away by a fierce winged serpent as his wife. So the sad parents prepared this funereal marriage for their unfortunate daughter. All the people of the town mourned and wept, and Psyche was escorted to the appointed mountain top and left to her fate.

5.) As she sat atop the mountain Psyche wept and trembled not knowing what was to come. *M* Suddenly a warm breath of wind caressed her neck and the invisible wind god Zephyrus lifted her up and away until she came down upon a soft fragrant valley far below. Psyche had forgotten all her fears here and fell asleep. When she woke, she saw a magnificent palace in the distance and hastened towards it. At the threshold of this unguarded and uninhabited mansion, she heard a *hurried* voice telling her: *entrance   empty*

6.) "All this is yours. Come bathe and refresh your tired limbs and prepare for dinner. We are here near you, but invisible and will satisfy your every wish and desire."

7.) The food was delicious and the bath so refreshing. While Psyche dined, she heard sweet melodious music, but could not see who was playing. As the day passed she began to feel *M* reassured that she would soon meet her husband. As night came she heard the sweet whispers of her husband's voice in her ears and realized that he was no monster of terror, but someone she had so desperately longed for. However with each dawn, her husband was gone, leaving Psyche alone in the giant palace.

James's Narrative

I walked towards the door that leads outside. I stood there for a second. Miguel walked up to me and said, "Are you going to see who made the team?" I said, "Yes." Then I asked him, "Do yu want to go up there together," and he said, "Sure." We walked upstairs, and the board was right next to Mr. Boles office. There was a big noisy crowd of middle school students in front of us. I asked Miguel, "How are we going to get through?" he said, "I don't know." I told him to follow me so we pushed our way through then saw the board. It was a brown board. There they were: the girls and boys Middle School Basketball teams. There was only 13 players on the team, and Miguel and I were one of them. We were happy so we went downstairs and told our friends we made the team.

Seminar Process Assessment

The Outcome of Change

Name: _Micha_

Date: _12/2/10_

Seminar Title: _Cupid and Psyche_

Ideas/Values: _Change, Metamorphosis, Decisions_

My goals for today's seminar are to (check two):

___	Yield to another in order to share talk time
√	Refer to the text in detail
√	Consider multiple points of view
___	Speak out of uncertainty

On a scale of one to five (one being not so good and five being excellent), I would rate myself as a _4_ in a relationship to my seminar goal. Because _I did refer to the text in detail but I only considered multiple points of view a cupple of times._

Micha's Inspectional and Analytical Read

Micha

Cupid and Psyche

(Prep-"Dr" not specific.)
(90)

1.) Once upon a time there was a king with three daughters, all were lovely, but the youngest named Psyche, excelled her sisters in beauty so much that she seemed like a goddess. The fame of her beauty spread far and wide and soon many people came to worship her. Meanwhile the real goddess of love, Venus (Aphrodite) became neglected as fewer people came to her temples to make offerings and pay her homage.

Over the top
gifts   *respect/honor*   *not cared for\mistreated*

2.) Venus grew jealous of Psyche and turned to her son Cupid (Eros) for help. She told Cupid to go and shoot Psyche with an arrow as to make her fall in love with the most vile and horrible creature on the earth. Cupid took up his bow and arrow, flew earthward, had one look at Psyche and was lost. No victim of his gold arrows was more deeply in love than he.

grass

3.) While everyone worshipped and admired Psyche, her beauty was so awesome that men were fearful to express their longing and desire for her or make plain their sentiments. Both her sisters though less lovely than Psyche had gotten married. So Psyche sat sad and solitary, only to be admired but not loved.

fortune teller
grieving

4.) Psyche's father began to suspect some curse had fallen on his youngest daughter, and went to the nearby town of Miletus to consult the oracle of Apollo. The oracle said that Psyche was to be dressed in clothes of mourning and placed on the summit of a mountain. There she would be taken away by a fierce winged serpent as his wife. So the sad parents prepared this funereal marriage for their unfortunate daughter. All the people of the town mourned and wept, and Psyche was escorted to the appointed mountain top and left to her fate.

5.) As she sat atop the mountain Psyche wept and trembled not knowing what was to come. Suddenly a warm breath of wind caressed her neck and the invisible wind god Zephyrus lifted her up and away until she came down upon a soft fragrant valley far below. Psyche had forgotten all her fears here and fell asleep. When she woke, she saw a magnificent palace in the distance and hastened towards it. At the threshold of this unguarded and uninhabited mansion, she heard a voice telling her:

speed up   *opening*   *empty*

6.) "All this is yours. Come bathe and refresh your tired limbs and prepare for dinner. We are here near you, but invisible and will satisfy your every wish and desire."

7.) The food was delicious and the bath so refreshing. While Psyche dined, she heard sweet melodious music, but could not see who was playing. As the day passed she began to feel reassured that she would soon meet her husband. As night came she heard the sweet whispers of her husband's voice in her ears and realized that he was no monster of terror, but someone she had so desperately longed for. However with each dawn, her husband was gone, leaving Psyche alone in the giant palace.

Micha's Narrative

We were all sad that our field trip was over. They were about to do a head count when I heard. Uhh! It was kyra. She sat up from the blue seat. I asked her what was wrong. She said. We forgot our shells in the meeting room! My eyes got bigger and wider and we popped up out of our seats. We ran to Mrs. Griffith. I was pushing through the teachers. but not to hard purpusly being careful and saying excuse me. She said we could go get the shells so we jumped off the bus. kyra told me to start running but I was scared that the bus might leave. I to come with me but she said she had to stay to make sure the bus would not leave I took off running and I was going fast and I could tell because I could hear the wind as I ran by. I guess I was going to fast because I ran right past the meeting area with the green roof and so I had to turn around. So once again I took off running. I got so excited because I could see the colorful shells. Some big, some small. and some round. Even though I was tired. I tried to pick them up but they would not fit in my pockets without breaking because of other stuff in my pocket. I could see that the bus driver was yelling at me. I could not understand her at first but she was jumping up and down. so that just made me go faster. As I got closer I could hear her She was shouting. Come on. HURRY. I was ready to fall down on the ground because I was so tired. but I could not give u now! I gave it all might and the bus was started and ready to go. I ran even faster. Before I knew it I was on the bus going home. Now. I remember my things when I go on field trips!

"Cupid and Psyche" Seminar Map

Sixth Grade

Text: "Cupid and Psyche"   Date: 8/24/10

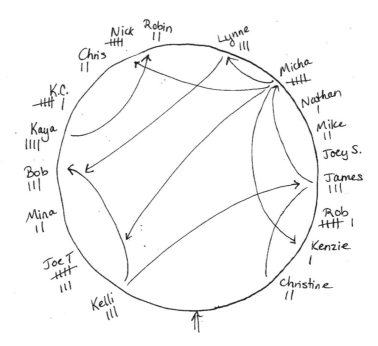

Grades for "Cupid and Psyche" Seminar

James:

> Pre-content: B
>
> Process: B
>
> Post-content: B
>
> Map: talked a good amount, cited text
>
> Overall grade for seminar: B

Micha:

> Pre-content: B
>
> Process: B
>
> Post-content: A
>
> Map: talked a good amount, cited text
>
> Overall grade for seminar: A

Self-Assessment Practices

As you can see, we advocate using these multiple data sets and a triangulated perspective in order to achieve the most valid measurement of the interrelated skills of speaking, listening, and thinking. Using the teacher map *alone* to "give a grade" is unfair both in terms of measurement and for the integrity of the practice. It is impossible for one person to track the full participation of a group of students' speaking, listening, and thinking. For that reason, the teacher's seminar map and notes represent only one, relatively small part of the data we use for assessment.

Authentic self-assessment is as important for developing the skills of speaking, listening, and thinking as the actual practice itself. Raising the students' awareness of what a good thinker and communicator does helps them master these skills. It may be that students need help in doing productive self-assessment and teachers are rightly concerned with this aspect of the seminar assessment process. This, however, opens up another possible teaching opportunity. In other words, a teacher can help a student set an appropriate personal goal, and if the post-process assessment seems off base, then the teacher should use his or her map to coach the student toward accurate, authentic reflection.

Measuring seminar participation before and after the discussion is not a matter of the teacher/facilitator *doing to* or *for* the student/participant. The student must help generate the feedback that will support learning. Then, students are engaged as active partners, becoming more aware of the different facets of discussion, and they are working to add to their own skill set. Each student is taking steps to becoming a well-rounded communicator and thinker.

Authentic self-assessment is as important for developing the skills of speaking, listening, and thinking as the actual practice itself.

The facilitator gives time and space for students to consider their own communication skills, both individually and collectively. The facilitator helps the assessment process by keeping the data organized so that it can be retrieved for future use. Students/participants use their written goals and self-assessment notes to identify skills relevant for them at the time and to plan more challenging goals over a series of discussions. The goal is steady student progress; however, it may take several practice discussions to achieve certain goals.

Over time, most if not all of the data from one seminar should be used to inform the next. Students should review goals and self-assessments that they made during previous seminars in order to set goals for the current seminar. Likewise, the teacher map from one seminar should inform group goals for the next seminar and perhaps some individual goal setting as well.

Finally, it is important to remember that there is more going on than can be captured by traditional means of assessment. When a group comes together in thoughtful dialogue, both the collective performance and the individual skills come from several layers of prior experience. For example, gender matters, as different ways of thinking and communicating for boys and girls are very much a social norm. Similarly, a participant's cultural background influences habits of reasoning, intuiting, and communicating. On any given day, an individual's unique mental, physical, and emotional state can make or break a dialogic effort.

This is all to say that teaching, learning, and assessing thoughtful dialogue is profoundly important and yet wonderfully complex. The many elements involved create something like a puzzle to be solved, particularly when we try to assess the thinking skills involved in a dynamic group dialogue. As difficult as it is, we believe that candid assessment is a fundamental part of the learning process and should always be focused on helping individual seminar participants improve their participation over time. After all, speaking, listening, and thinking are the most basic of skills.

Chapter Seven in Sum

In order to consistently assess an individual's participation in the seminar process, the teacher/facilitator must assess that individual's speaking, listening, *and* thinking skills.

In order to do this in a valid way, the teacher must collect at least three kinds of data from three separate artifacts:

- ♦ student pre- and post-seminar process documents

- ♦ student post-seminar content writing (or other form of expression)

- ♦ teacher seminar map and notes

We advocate weighting these three artifacts in the grading process by assigning 45 percent credit to the student process documents, 45 percent to the student writing, and 10 percent to the teacher map/notes. Obviously, this scale places 90 percent of the final value on student self-assessment (coached by the teacher), but this system is the only valid way to assess all aspects of seminar participation.

Candid and collaborative assessment is a fundamental part of the learning process. We believe Paideia Seminar assessment should be focused on helping individual participants improve their speaking, listening, and thinking skills over time.

8

Socrates Teaching Thinking: A Secondary Seminar

"[Plato's] dialogues—and particularly the early ones—set forth problems which often they do not solve; in the dialogues, each different character stands for some different point of view; thus, Plato's works are dramas of intellectual conflict, whose vividness and value to the reader lie frequently in their evocation of the actual history of a mind, candidly facing the confusions of the problems, and struggling toward some solution."

—Raphael Demos

We are often asked what the finished product looks like. What is a mature seminar experience like for both facilitator and participants? Rather than answer that question with an ideal that is so far removed from reality as to seem unattainable, we will close by reproducing for you another seminar that is real as well as ideal.

In a small Southern city, there is a K–12 magnet school dedicated to the Paideia philosophy. The school is located in a historic structure near downtown; we will call it the School for Liberal Arts and Sciences.[1] If a child enters the school in kindergarten, he or she will experience a school-wide Paideia Seminar at least every other week for thirteen years, this in addition to the many seminars he or she will experience in their regular classes. We tell you this in order to prepare you for what you are about to read.

---

1 The name of the school has been changed to protect the privacy of teachers and students. The seminar described here is a compilation; however, the elements described in this chapter are quite common in a seminar at this level.

The Meno: Analyzing a Socratic Dialogue

Seniors at the School for Liberal Arts and Sciences can take a Survey of the Great Ideas as an elective course. In this course, they study two to four thematic units based on ideas and values that they themselves choose from the list of 103 Great Ideas published by Mortimer Adler and his colleagues at Encyclopedia Britannica in the 1950s. The seminar we are about to describe for you is a capstone event in a thematic study of the concept of "wisdom"; the text for the seminar is an excerpt from Plato's *The Meno*.[2] There are twenty-nine seniors in Ms. Boyer's Senior Seminar class. This particular Paideia Seminar is taking place at the end of the first semester during the class period normally devoted to reviewing for the semester exam. On the day of the exam, the students will write an in-class essay in response to the prompt they are given at the end of the seminar.

An experienced facilitator, Ms. Boyer has carefully integrated all four literacy skills—reading, speaking, listening, and writing—into her seminar plan for *The Meno*. She planned to have her students read the text three times prior to the seminar: first, to inspect it quickly; second, to read it aloud with two classmates; and third, with a graphic organizer in hand, to search for connections. During the discussion itself, which was scheduled to take place on Wednesday, the review day prior to the start of exams, she intended to emphasize rigorous process skills. Of course, the exam itself would consist of an in-class essay to be outlined after the seminar discussion.

Ms. Boyer began the planning process knowing she wanted her students to consider the following ideas among others: *questioning, thinking, truth,* and *wisdom*.[3] In particular, she wanted her students to discuss the nature of thinking as a search for truth. In the two weeks prior to the seminar itself, she went through four drafts of her seminar plan, writing and rewriting her questions, always conscious of the order in which she anticipated asking them as well as the wording of the questions themselves. For the entire semester, she had stressed clarity, coherence, and sophistication in her students' thinking and writing, and she had told them repeatedly that their exam essays would be graded on these criteria. She planned to emphasize these characteristics through the process skills she would suggest for the seminar.

---

2 The actual text for this seminar is approximately seven pages from the Benjamin Jowett translation (itself a modern classic) of *The Meno*, the pages covering Socrates' interview of the slave boy from Meno's household and the reflections on learning and thinking that follow immediately after. The text and a version of Ms. Boyer's seminar plan appear in Appendix C.

3 This excerpt from *The Meno* is most often used as a math seminar, in which students discuss problem solving among other things. The big ideas can include: approximation, geometry, mathematics, reason, square root. It is interesting to note here, that even though Ms. Boyer wasn't focusing on mathematics, the students did take the conversation there for a significant period of time.

A fan of Mortimer Adler's *How to Read a Book*, Ms. Boyer fully appreciates the value in multiple readings of a rich text. For homework on Monday evening prior to the Wednesday seminar, she asked her students to do a quick "inspectional" read of the text, using three colors of highlighter ink to mark the speakers' names in the dialogue: blue for Socrates, pink for Meno, and yellow for the slave boy. On Tuesday, in class, she divided the students into groups of three and asked them to read the text aloud, with each of the three students reading one of the parts. During the last fifteen minutes of class, she asked them to work in their groups to list adjectives describing each of the three characters; she thinks of this work as the "analytical" reading, following the previous "inspectional" reading. For homework on Tuesday night, she asked the students to read the text for a third time, this time while filling out the following graphic organizer (a type of "syntopical" reading), shown in Figure 8.1.[4] Their assignment was to look for connections: text to self, text to world, text to text. In Ms. Boyer's mind, the last category was especially important at this point in the semester, because she wanted her students to see connections between *The Meno* and earlier seminar texts related to "wisdom."

Figure 8.1. Graphic Organizer: Making Coherent Connections

Reread the excerpt from *The Meno*. This time, look for important connections and record them below. In the first category, record elements in the text you relate to personally; in the second, record connections between the text and the outside world; and in the third, record connections between this text and others we have read during our study of "wisdom."

Quote from text (note page #)	...is connected to:
Text to Self:	This reminds me of…
Text to World:	This reminds me of something I heard/saw…
Text to Text:	This reminds me of something else I've read…

---

4 For further discussion of this type of reading strategy, see Chris Tovani's *I Read It, but I Don't Get It: Comprehension Strategies for Adolescent Readers,* as well as Stephanie Harvey and Anne Goudvis' *Strategies That Work: Teaching Comprehension to Enhance Understanding.*

During the week of the seminar, Ms. Boyer posted a list of the "wisdom" seminar texts on the whiteboard for ready reference. Since the first week in September, her class has participated in a full seminar cycle on each of the following texts listed on the board:

"The Allegory of the Cave" from *The Republic* (Plato)

Ecclesiastes, Chapter 3 ("The Preacher")

"Community" from *The Meditations* (Marcus Aurelius)

Head of a Man (painting by Paul Klee)

"Truth and Tact" from the *Tao te Ching* (Lao Tzu)

"Of Wisdom for a Man's Self" (Francis Bacon)

Migrant Mother (photograph by Dorothea Lange)

On the day of the seminar, all twenty-nine students are present (knowing they need the seminar discussion to help them write their exam essay). They take their accustomed places in the seminar circle in Ms. Boyer's room. After a brief review of the background information on Plato and *The Meno*, she reminds the students that during the seminar they will discuss the following ideas (among others): learning, questioning, thinking, truth, and wisdom. She then begins her pre-seminar process ritual. First, she reminds them of her role (asking questions and taking notes) versus their role (sharing their ideas through statements and questions; listening with an open mind; agreeing and disagreeing graciously). She sets for them a group goal of "being as clear as possible in our use of language" during the discussion. She justifies this by reminding them that they will eventually be graded on the clarity of their thought in their exam essays. She then asks them to choose a goal to focus on during the seminar, thereby challenging them to improve on previous seminar participation. She has them choose from these process goals:

♦ to make specific references to the text

♦ to make connections between ideas

♦ to identify contradictions

♦ to keep an open mind

These process goals are much more sophisticated than the ones with which the class began the semester; as her students have grown in their participation skills, Ms. Boyer has increased the level of the challenge. In addition, this particular list of skills is designed to help the students both speak and write with clarity ("make specific references to the text"), coherence ("make connections" and "identify contradictions"), and sophistication (again "make connections" and "identify contradictions").

Ms. Boyer then asks her opening question, reading it slowly twice to give her students a chance to fully comprehend it: "At the beginning of the semester, we read an excerpt from Plato's *Republic* that has come to be called 'The Allegory of the Cave.' Our text today is another excerpt from a longer work by Plato; what do you think would be a good title for this text?" The students know that they will each have to give a title before Ms. Boyer opens the floor to spontaneous discussion. As they begin to re-examine the text in search of a telling phrase or image, Ms. Boyer jots their names down on her seminar "map," or seating chart.

As she fills in the students' names on her seating chart (Figure 8.2), Ms. Boyer reflects on the variety of personalities and styles in the circle: Lory and Jerome, who seldom speak and who are working on their ability to share their ideas; Jametta, Tim, and C.J., all of whom love to argue and who are working on their ability to listen as well as talk. And then there is Jamal, who is perfectly willing to share his thoughts as long as no one contradicts him, at which point he tends to pout for the remainder of the seminar. Jamal isn't alone in this reaction; Adam and Raymond don't like to be contradicted either. All three are working on their ability to listen to others with an open mind. Ivey and Henry love to talk, but sometimes it is a struggle to relate what they are saying to the text; their practice involves learning to stay on topic by citing the text whenever they speak. Finally, Ms. Boyer realizes with a smile that every student in the circle except one has to work on being precise in their use of language. Only Thomas, her one completely addicted reader, is careful to define his words when he uses them and asks others to do the same. His classmates call him the "word nerd," and he has enough style to adopt the phrase as his own; it is written on the back of his "name tent," the folded index card that marks each student's place in the circle. Their first names are written in block letters on the front of the name tent (it was what Ms. Boyer used to adjust their seating order and to identify them when she videotaped discussions), and their evolving process goals are noted on the back, where they can see them.

The strongest possible combination of thinking, listening, and speaking skills—that is the goal that each student seeks—and each student has his or her current challenge to work on.

The opening question is: *"What do you think would be a good title for this excerpt from* The Meno?" As she glances around the circle one last time, Ms. Boyer realizes that most of the students are ready to offer their initial responses. Ms. Boyer asks first for a brief response from each participant—just the proposed title—with explanation to come later. Jametta volunteers to start (no surprise) and she offers "Socrates and the Slave Boy" as a title. Ms. Boyer nods to Will, who sits to Jametta's left, and he suggests "Recollection." Carol follows with "Socrates and the Boy," and then it is Thomas' turn. After a pause, he whispers "Thinking Is Recollection." And so on around the circle.

Figure 8.2. Ms. Boyer's Seating Plan

Senior Great Ideas

Text: The "Meno"   Date: December 13, 2010

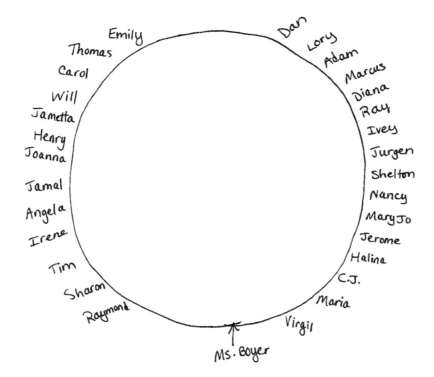

At one point Jurgen suggests "Socrates and the Student Teacher," and everyone laughs because Ms. Boyer's student teacher from the local university is observing and taking notes. "Who's the student teacher in the dialogue, Jurgen?" Ms. Boyer asks. "Meno, of course," Jurgen replies; more laughter. Halina, the best math student in the class, says the title should be "The Square Within the Square," and before Ms. Boyer can stop her, adds, "this really is all about math, you know," and points to the diagram in the text (Figure 8.3).

Figure 8.3. The Square Within the Square

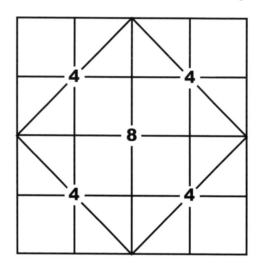

After every student has offered a title (even Jerome has managed to whisper "The Boy"), Ms. Boyer reminds the students that clarity in the use of language is their group goal and then opens the floor to spontaneous discussion so they can explain their suggested titles. Lory, one of the more introverted students, responds to Ms. Boyer's pre-seminar coaching by beginning the conversation. She had followed Will in naming the piece "Recollection," and she points out that the excerpt begins with Meno asking Socrates to explain why "learning is only a process of recollection." "It's like Plato's giving us the title," she adds quietly. Will quickly agrees with Lory. After a few other students have spoken, Halina, who seldom talks a lot during seminar, speaks up to defend "The Square Within the Square." Two other students had named the text "Square Root," and Halina says, "I have to disagree with Dan and Ivey. It's not really about square root. That's not what Socrates is asking the Boy. He's asking him what square is half the size of the larger square, not what square multiplied by itself will equal the larger square." Most of the class stares blankly at Halina. Ms. Boyer suggests Emily raise the screen that was partially blocking the whiteboard. When she does, the students can see the same diagram drawn on the board that Halina referred to earlier. "Okay, Halina," she says. "This is a chance for us to define our terms more clearly.

See if you can explain to all of us, me included, what you mean when you say, 'the issue here is not Square Root but The Square Within the Square'"?

Halina gets up and goes to the board. She points to the lower right quadrant of the diagram and then to the other three quadrants in turn. She says as she does so: "This is the diagram that Socrates draws in the dirt, starting on page 6. He draws four squares, each of which contains four square feet. Together they total square feet, as you can see from counting the total number of squares. His question to the Boy is what size square contains half this amount of space, or eight square feet. Once he starts drawing, he turns it into a problem in geometry."

Suddenly, Dan interrupts her. "Oh, I see what you're saying. The diagonal line isn't the square root of four, it's the side of a square that contains half as much space as a square that's four units long on each side." Halina nods emphatically. Dan joins Halina at the board. He picks up a red marker and uses it to outline the diamond within the larger square. Then he uses the marker to count the number of squares and half squares inside the diamond. "What'd you get?" Halina asks him. "Eight, of course," he mutters. "So…?" she urges him. "So, the square in red is exactly half the size of the square in black." "And that's the solution to the problem," Halina adds for emphasis.

After the two sit back down, Ms. Boyer asks: "So, did Socrates solve the problem, or did the Boy?" A lively debate emerges between Sharon, Jamal, and Mary Jo on the one hand (who argue that Socrates leads the Boy to the solution by drawing the diagram and asking leading questions) and Will, Diana, and C.J. on the other (who argue that the Boy works out the solution for himself, stimulated by Socrates' questions). After a few minutes of back-and-forth, Emily interrupts the debate to say: "I want to identify this as a contradiction. Either Socrates solves the problem or the Boy does, one or the other, and it seems like…" She gestures vaguely at the whole circle. "Like we're contradicting each other."

"Thank you, Emily," Ms. Boyer recognizes her. "Is there a third possibility, then? Something that is neither Socrates alone nor the Boy alone?"

"How about both?" Thomas asks.

"That's ridiculous," Jamal says. "Two people can't solve a math problem together."

"I disagree," Diana says quickly. "I disagree with Jamal. When my sister helps me with my math homework, sometimes we have to talk about a problem in order for her to remember enough to show me how to work it. I think I can see what Thomas is saying. Two people working together."

Ms. Boyer notices that Jamal has crossed his arms stubbornly and is staring at his desk, refusing to make eye contact with Thomas or Diana.

The seminar continues in this vein for a while, with a number of students joining the discussion of Socrates' contribution versus the Boy's contribution. Mary Jo even points out that Socrates may have needed the Boy to work through the problem as much as the Boy needed Socrates, admitting that she's changed her mind after hearing what Diana and Thomas have to say. Jamal still doesn't speak.

Eventually, Ms. Boyer adds another question to the mix. "Go back to page 5," she directs the participants. "Socrates says to Meno about the Boy: 'Do you see…what advances he has made?…He did not know at first, and he does not know now, what is the side of a figure of eight feet: but then he thought he knew, and answered confidently as if he knew, and had no difficulty; now he has a difficulty, and neither knows nor fancies that he knows.' Why do you think Socrates calls this an advance?"

After a moment, Virgil says, "The boy has made progress because he realizes that he doesn't know the answer."

"I know how he feels," Ray says. "I don't know the answer in math either." Laughter at Ray's rueful shrug.

"But it's more than that," Halina says. "It's more specific than that. He knows his first two answers won't work, and he knows that the real answer lies somewhere in between. He understands…something."

Thomas speaks for the first time since the opening question. "He understands the nature of the problem much better even though he doesn't know the answer."

A discussion ensues over whether it's more important to understand the problem or to know the answer. Eventually Jametta says that in math class, it's more important to know the answer but in life, it's more important to understand the problem. The students seem more-or-less satisfied with this generalization.

Ms. Boyer glances at her watch; there are fifteen minutes left in the class, and there are at least two more questions she wants to ask. She asks the first question. "Based on this text, how do you think Socrates would define *thinking*?"

There's a long pause. Then, surprisingly, Lory is again first to speak. "He would define it as *recollection*. He pretty much says so."

Ms. Boyer: "What do you think he means, though? Thinking is recollection?"

Lory glances at Thomas, anxious for his help. But before Thomas can speak, Will jumps in. "Maybe he means that the answers are inside us somehow. Not that we once had them all memorized and just forgot but rather that…."

Thomas joins in when Will pauses. "I agree with Lory and Will. I wonder what the original word was in Greek, if it meant something other than just recollection. Because I think Socrates is saying that we each have the potential inside us to figure things out, to think for ourselves, but something has to unlock the potential."

"What unlocks the potential?" Maria asks, before Ms. Boyer has a chance to.

Thomas shakes his head. "I'm not sure."

Jamal speaks for the first time since he became frustrated early on. "The questions unlock the potential. I mean, isn't it obvious? Socrates goes around drawing pictures in the dirt and asking questions."

Nods and general agreement around the circle. "It's all about the questions." "The questions are the key."

Then Jurgen: "You all laughed at me when I said the title should be 'Socrates and the Student Teacher,' but now you see I'm right. Socrates is teaching Meno how to ask questions by demonstrating on the Slave Boy."

There's a long pause, and then: "You know," Jametta says. "I never thought I'd hear myself say this, but I agree with Jurgen. I think he's on to something. Maybe Socrates is teaching us all to ask questions. The questions are more important than the answers."

"Is that part of his definition of thinking?" Ms. Boyer asks.

"Maybe it's the most important part of all," Tim says. (Ms. Boyer notes that this is the first time he's spoken and she's grateful. He usually tries to dominate the discussion.) "Maybe questioning is the key to thinking."

"Then I have one last *question* for you," Ms. Boyer says. "What did you learn from this text and our discussion? Learn about thinking or learn about yourselves as thinkers?" The students recognize this as her closing question, and they pause for a moment to consider.

Raymond, who is sitting beside Ms. Boyer, shifts in his seat uncomfortably, and then speaks while staring down at his desk. "I learned that we're all like the Slave Boy. We all have that potential that Thomas was talking about even if we don't make very good grades or if some people look down on us."

Angela, who is the only student who hasn't spoken to this point, finally joins the fray. "I learned that sometimes it takes a shock to make us really think. Socrates and Meno keep referring to the 'torpedo shock' that Socrates has given the Boy. By making him doubt what he thought he knew."

"Is that a good thing? That shock?" Ms. Boyer asks.

"Socrates and Meno think it is. Socrates keeps asking the Boy questions, over and over, endlessly."

"Like you do us!" Jametta adds. And everyone laughs.

"But there's something else," Thomas says suddenly, sensing that Ms. Boyer is about to end the seminar. "There's something else in Socrates' last speech. He says we must 'seek to know what we do not know' and that he is 'ready to fight' for the right to know. You asked us what Socrates believes thinking is. I believe that for him, it's the search for the truth, no matter the consequences...."

The students turn to look at Ms. Boyer expectantly. "I think we can stop with that," she says.

There is an audible group sigh, as there almost always is when Ms. Boyer calls an end to a seminar. The students know they still have to debrief, but the real work, the speaking and listening and thinking, is almost over for the day.

After a moment, Ms. Boyer asks the students to first consider their group goal. "We set ourselves the task of 'using language as precisely as possible.' On a scale of one to five, how do you think we did?" The students raise their hands to vote, showing one to five fingers (one signifying "awful" and five "supreme") in response. Most of them are voting in the four to five range. "Okay, you know the drill. Why do you think we were a four or a five today?"

Will points at Halina. "It helped us focus when Halina forced us to differentiate between square root and one square that is half the area of another square. It wasn't fun, necessarily, but she made us think about what the words meant." Further discussion, and then Ivey says: "It always helps when you ask us about a specific word, like *recollection* or *thinking*. What does Socrates mean by *thinking*? That forces us to pay attention to how that one word is being used in the text." After a moment, Dan adds: "I also like the way we were careful when we differentiated between 'understanding the problem' and 'knowing the answer.' I never really thought about that before and it turns out there is a big difference."

Realizing she has only five minutes left before the bell, Ms. Boyer pushes her students to consider one more question. "How did you do with your individual process goals ("make connections," "identify contradictions," etc.)? Volunteers…?" Jamal slowly raised his hand. "My personal goal was to keep an open mind," he said ruefully. "And I failed pretty miserably. I got so pissed when Diana disagreed with me that I didn't listen to a word she or anybody else said for a long time. Sorry, Diana." "And next time?" Ms. Boyer prompts him. "In the next seminar, I'm going to listen, *especially* when somebody disagrees with me!" Out of the corner of her eye, Ms. Boyer can see Diana smiling at Jamal.

After a few more minutes of "true confessions," as the students call them, first Ray and then Emily ask to see the seminar map. Emily: "Since we were so focused on making all kinds of connections, including contradictions, what does the map say about how we did?" Ms. Boyer places her seminar map (Figure 8.4) on the document camera at the front of the room and projects it onto a blank section of wall. The students gasp and then cheer; the center of the seminar map is criss-crossed with dozens of lines ending in arrows, Ms. Boyer's symbol for when one student refers to another's statement or idea, even when disagreeing. She applauds along with them because this seminar was remarkable for the extent to which the students consistently wove their comments together into something larger than the sum of its parts.

Figure 8.4. Ms. Boyer's Seminar Map

Senior Great Ideas

Text: The "Meno"   Date: December 13, 2010

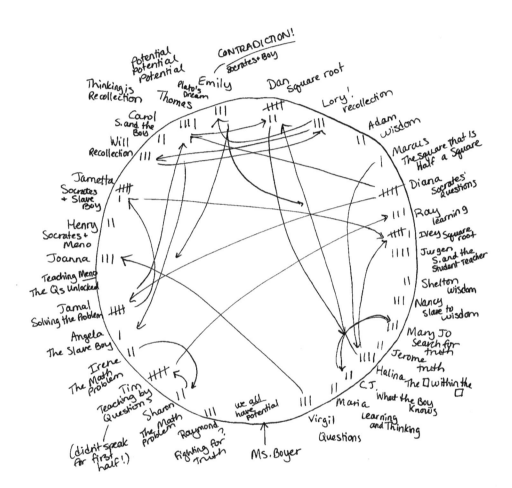

"You deserved that round of applause," she says as the bell rings. "You were magnificent today. Now, let's only hope that all these connections result in clarity and coherence when you write the exam on Friday. The blue sheet of paper on the shelf by the door is your essay assignment for the exam. No mysteries, no surprises, and it's impossible to cheat unless you write the essay in advance. I'll be here all day tomorrow, so stop by if you need clarification on anything." This last is said over the sound of the bell ending the period and the rough and tumble of kids jamming books and papers into backpacks and flooding through the door out into the hallway. Only Thomas, the "word nerd," pauses, as he always does, to formally shake her hand. "Thank you," he says. "Very good discussion." "It was indeed," Ms. Boyer admits. "Maybe our best so far."

When she bends to pick up a stray sheet of blue paper, blown to the floor by the river of students passing out of the room, she rereads their assignment, curious to see how it sounds in light of the discussion they just had.

> Please respond to the following prompt by writing for no more than one hour. Write a personal definition in several paragraphs of one of the following terms: *learning, questioning, thinking, truth, wisdom.* Please refer in detail to the excerpt from *The Meno* and at least two other works that we have studied and discussed during our unit on "wisdom." (The list will be on the board during the exam.) You may bring your copies of the texts you wish to use to class along with your notes. The only thing that I ask is that you not write the essay in advance. Your definition will be graded on its clarity, coherence, and sophistication.

"Clarity, coherence, sophistication," she repeats to herself. "Clarity, coherence, sophistication." Since the next period of the day is her planning period, she has time to reflect on the seminar she has just led. She gathers her copy of the text (now covered with notes from the discussion), her seminar plan (covered with edits for the next time she leads the same seminar), and her seminar map. When she clips all of these materials into the binder that houses her Seminar Facilitation Portfolio, she pauses to compare the map of this seminar to the very first one she led with these students in August. She realizes with gratification just how far they have come: The talk turns are much more evenly distributed around the circle than they were before, and the evidence of students making connections between ideas has increased dramatically. Even though these students are the products of years of seminar practice, they are continuing to grow in response to her demands that they become increasingly clear in their use of language and that they search for connections. Even Jamal's admission that he doesn't have the intellectual flexibility to respond well to contradiction is a sign of growth. He has recognized without her prompting what is expected of him as a mature seminar participant: "To listen, *especially* when somebody disagrees with me." She realizes that open-mindedness should probably be the group goal for the first few seminars in the second semester, giving the entire class the opportunity to discuss in detail what open-mindedness looks and sounds like. She writes detailed notes to herself, knowing that she will need them after winter break when it comes time to plan. Before closing her portfolio, she thumbs through the dozens of pages of plans, texts, and notes. With a smile, she realizes that her 29 seniors are growing up—they are learning to think.

If you were to interview Ms. Boyer about her dedication to the seminar process, to press her about the value of communication and thinking skills in an educational environment ruled at almost every level by standardized testing, she might quote for you a book by Robert Maynard Hutchins written just after World War II. The book is titled *The Great Conversation*, and it serves as the introductory volume to The Great Books of the Western World. In the first chapter of *The Great Conversation*, Hutchins writes:

> The liberally educated man [or woman] has a mind that can operate well in all fields. He may be a specialist in one field. But he can understand anything important that is said in any field and can see and use the light that it sheds upon his own. The liberally educated man is at home in the world of ideas and in the world of practical affairs, too, because he understands the relation of the two. He may not be at home in the world of practical affairs in the sense of liking the life he finds about him; but he will be at home in that world in the sense that he understands it. He may even derive from his liberal education some conception of the difference between a bad world and a good one and some notion of the ways in which one might be turned into the other. (p. 4)

Ms. Boyer and hundreds of teachers like her are dedicated to teaching thinking skills within the laboratory of the Paideia Seminar—stressing over and over again in a cyclical way the component skills of speaking and listening (as well as reading and writing)—until their students show measurable gains in clarity, coherence, and sophistication. Until, they hope, their students are prepared to take the life tests that will come long after their schooling is over.

These teachers know that, on some very fundamental level, thinking is literacy and literacy is thinking, regardless of the discipline being taught. They are dedicated to exercising their own minds as well as those of their students. As a result, they are the master teachers that we all aspire to become.

Chapter Eight in Sum

A mature seminar with experienced participants led by a skilled facilitator illustrates just how powerful the process can be. It shows how practice in the four basic literacy skills—reading, writing, speaking, and listening—nurtures critical and creative thinking.

For all the reasons illustrated here, teaching thinking through seminar discussion leads to lifelong literacy and lifelong learning.

Appendix A

Things Worth Talking About

*"An idea that is not dangerous is unworthy of
being called an idea at all."*
—Oscar Wilde

The Paideia Seminar was first described by philosopher-educator Mortimer Adler in a series of books published during the 1980s, primarily *The Paideia Proposal* (1982) and *The Paideia Program* (1984). From the beginning, Adler described the Seminar as a form of teaching and learning that complemented didactic instruction and academic coaching. It was intended to teach the conceptual understanding of ideas and values.

Simply defined, an idea is a thought, mental image, or notion. A value is an idea that is considered desirable or worthy for its own sake. Experienced seminar facilitators typically identify three to five important ideas that guide them in choosing a text and drafting questions.

The next page provides a list of sample ideas and values that we have drawn from two sources: Adler's list of 103 "Great Ideas" derived while indexing *The Great Books of the Western World*, and M. Scott Peck's list of common values from his *Abounding Grace* (2000). It is by no means a complete list, but it serves as a convenient starting point when planning a seminar.

These ideas and values have generated powerful dialogue for thousands of years because they are fundamentally ambiguous. Figuratively speaking, they are more like questions than statements, and so generate the multiple points of view that lead through discussion to more sophisticated understanding.

Ideas and Values for Discussion

Angel

Animal

Aristocracy

Art

Astronomy

Beauty

Being

Cause

Chance

Citizen

Constitution

Courage

Custom and Convention

Compassion

Courtesy

Deduction

Definition

Democracy

Desire

Dialectic

Duty

Education

Equality

Element

Emotion

Estimation

Eternity

Evolution

Experience

Faith

Family

History

Honor

Hypothesis

Immortality

Induction

Infinity

Judgment

Justice

Knowledge

Labor

Language

Law

Liberty

Life and Death

Logic

Love

Man

Mathematics

Matter

Mechanics

Medicine

Memory and Imagination

Soul

Metaphysics

Mind

Monarchy

Nature

Necessity and Contingency

Number

Oligarchy

One and Many

Physics

Principle

Progress

Prophecy

Proportion

Prudence

Punishment

Purity

Quality

Quantity

Reasoning

Relation

Religion

Respect

Revolution

Rhetoric

Same and Other

Science

Sense

Sign and Symbol

Sin

Slavery

Space

State

Strength

Temperance

Theology

Time

Truth

Tyranny

Universal and Particular

Fate	Opinion	Virtue and Vice
Form	Opposition	War and Peace
God	Perseverance	Wealth
Good and Evil	Philosophy	Will
Government	Pleasure and Pain	Wisdom
Habit	Poetry	World
Happiness	Power	

With these and similar ideas and values in mind, a prospective seminar facilitator can choose a text that is more likely to inspire a creative seminar discussion. Texts can vary widely in form or type from print to non-print. For example, a seminar text may be a poem, a painting, a chart, a story, an essay, a word problem, a map, or…the list goes on and on. But all good seminar texts have in some measure the following characteristics:

- ♦ They are rich in ideas and values.
- ♦ They offer complexity and challenge.
- ♦ They are relevant to those involved.
- ♦ They are fundamentally ambiguous.

These are the characteristics that generate multiple perspectives from seminar participants, multiple perspectives that lead in turn to the more sophisticated juxtaposition and merger of those points of view. In short, these ideas—and the texts that convey them—are worth talking about.

Appendix B

Questions Worth Asking

"Yet the great issues are there. What is our destiny?
What is a good life? How can we achieve a good society?
What can we learn to guide us through the mazes of the
future from history, philosophy, literature, and the fine arts?"
—Robert Maynard Hutchins

The primary task of a seminar facilitator is to ask evocative questions, drive the discussion first by engaging the participants and then by inspiring their thinking. While the best seminar questions can seem simple at times, there is an art to both composing and asking them.

Although questions will vary depending on the text under discussion and the participants involved, there is a consistent set of characteristics that define a strong question. It is always open-ended, thought-provoking, and clear.

All seminar questions are open-ended in that they are designed to elicit numerous correct responses. To be correct, a participant's response need only be on topic (often but not always referring directly to the text). The openness of seminar questions invites multiple perspectives and allows a much wider range of participation than do more closed, traditional questions.

Good seminar questions are also thought-provoking: first by sparking numerous responses and then by requiring participants to synthesize those responses. Often, facilitators ask those in the circle to examine the assumptions and implications of their own statements; and as the seminar proceeds, they often ask that participants exhibit increasingly complex thinking.

Finally, all good questions are clear. Participants should understand immediately what is being asked. Often, clarity comes with simplicity; the fewer the number of words in a question, the more effective it usually is. When experienced facilitators find themselves needing to ask a more complex question, they are careful to preface it adequately, speak slowly, and repeat it at least twice. In other words, ask a complex question in a clear and simple way.

When you examine the sample seminar plans in Appendix C, you will see that the questions are divided into three categories: opening, core, and closing.

Typically, a seminar leader asks only one opening question. This question is designed to get participants to identify the ideas and values in the text they are most interested in discussing. A good opening question is usually very easy to answer. (For example, "What is the most important word in the speech?" "What detail do you notice first in the painting?") It requires that the participants look closely at the text in order to respond, and invites a wide range of possible responses.

Core questions, of which there are usually three to five in a typical plan, are designed to have participants analyze the text in detail. They require that those in the circle study what the text has to say before allowing themselves to branch out into their own reactions to the text. (For example, "Why do you think the author chose that specific image?" "How is the message of the first paragraph related to the message of the second?") Early core questions are often designed to elicit multiple perspectives, while later core questions often ask participants to juxtapose and even synthesize those responses based on the text.

Closing questions, usually one or, at the most, two in any seminar, ask the participants to personalize the ideas and values under discussion. In other words, now that they have analyzed what the text has to say, participants are being asked to respond in a more personal way to the ideas and values under discussion. (For example, "If you were that character, how would you have responded? Why?" "Which of these two paintings would you choose to illustrate your personal journal? Why?")

It is important to note that any good seminar plan is only a draft, not a script. Experienced facilitators ask many, sometimes most, of their questions based on what they hear participants say during the course of the discussion. They do this in order to tailor their questions such that they inspire these particular participants to juxtapose and synthesize the ideas they find most compelling. In order to do this, a facilitator has to listen carefully, take good notes, and then craft a follow-up question that invites participants to build on what has already been said. As student participants become more comfortable with the seminar process, it is perfectly natural for them to begin to ask thought-provoking questions as well; in fact, they should be encouraged to do so. Often, the best questions emerge from the participants themselves.

Finally, whether the questions are planned or spontaneous, whether they come from a facilitator or participant, they are about ideas. Not just any ideas, but the fundamental human concerns that have haunted us as a species for thousands of years. As Robert Maynard Hutchins put it in *The Great Conversation*: "Yet the great issues are there. What is our destiny? What is a good life? How can we achieve a good society?" The ideas that haunt us do so because they are themselves not answers but questions.

Appendix C

Sample Seminar Texts and Plans

*"And so…we have at last arrived at
the hymn of dialectic only."*
—Plato (Book VII, *The Republic*)

Good seminar texts consistently inspire rich conversations because they evoke multiple ideas and are ambiguous enough to inspire multiple perspectives. In a similar fashion, good seminar plans bring the participants to the discussion well prepared to take full advantage of the text; provide an outline of evocative, open-ended questions for the seminar proper; and then provide multiple opportunities for debriefing the process and extending understanding after the fact. To accomplish all this, good seminar plans contain five sections:

1) pre-seminar content guidelines to guide the participants' "reading" of the text

2) pre-seminar process strategies to help participants speak and listen with focus and clarity

3) seminar questions (opening, core, closing) that are open-ended and clear

4) post-seminar process strategies for debriefing speaking and listening skills

5) post-seminar content assignment(s) that ask participants to extend their understanding.

You will see all of these elements in the plans that are included along with the sample texts in this appendix.

The six texts and plans contained here are given in order of increasing complexity. The first pair are probably most appropriate for elementary grades, the second pair for middle grades, and the third pair for high school and beyond. They represent a range of subject areas; indeed, most can be used in multiple subject areas. One of the texts (the excerpt from Mill's *On Liberty*) has explicitly to do with how dialogue nurtures thinking. The six texts and plans we have chosen to include are:

- "The Elves and the Shoemaker" (1814 folk tale) collected by the Grimm brothers

- *Washington Crossing the Delaware* (1851 painting) by Emanual Leutze

- "Axioms, or Laws of Motion" (1687) by Sir Isaac Newton

- "Tell all the Truth but tell it slant" (c. 1868 poem) by Emily Dickinson

- excerpt from *The Meno* (c. 387 B.C. dialogue) by Plato

- excerpt from Chapter Two, "On the Liberty of Thought and Discussion," from *On Liberty* (1859 treatise) by John Stuart Mill

SEMINAR PLAN

The Elves and the Shoemaker (1814)

Jacob and Wilhelm Grimm

There was once a shoemaker, who, through no fault of his own, became so poor that at last he had nothing left but just enough leather to make one pair of shoes. He cut out the shoes at night, so as to set to work upon them next morning; and as he had a good conscience, he laid himself quietly down in his bed, committed himself to heaven, and fell asleep. In the morning, after he had said his prayers, and was going to get to work, he found the pair of shoes made and finished, and standing on his table. He was very much astonished, and could not tell what to think, and he took the shoes in his hand to examine them more nearly; and they were so well made that every stitch was in its right place, just as if they had come from the hand of a master-workman.

Soon after a purchaser entered, and as the shoes fitted him very well, he gave more than the usual price for them, so that the shoemaker had enough money to buy leather for two more pairs of shoes. He cut them out at night, and intended to set to work the next morning with fresh spirit; but that was not to be, for when he got up they were already finished, and a customer even was not lacking, who gave him so much money that he was able to buy leather enough for four new pairs. Early next morning he found the four pairs also finished, and so it always happened; whatever he cut out in the evening was worked up by the morning, so that he was soon in the way of making a good living, and in the end became very well to do.

One night, not long before Christmas, when the shoemaker had finished cutting out, and before he went to bed, he said to his wife,

"How would it be if we were to sit up to-night and see who it is that does us this service?"

His wife agreed, and set a light to burn. Then they both hid in a corner of the room, behind some coats that were hanging up, and then they began to watch. As soon as it was midnight they saw come in two neatly-formed naked little men, who seated themselves before the shoemaker's table, and took up the work that was already prepared, and began to stitch, to pierce, and to hammer so cleverly and quickly with their little fingers that the shoemaker's eyes could scarcely follow them, so full of wonder was he. And they never left off until everything was finished and was standing ready on the table, and then they jumped up and ran off.

The next morning the shoemaker's wife said to her husband, "Those little men have made us rich, and we ought to show ourselves grateful. With all their running about, and having nothing to cover them, they must be very cold. I'll tell you what; I will make little shirts, coats, waistcoats, and breeches for them, and knit each of them a pair of stockings, and you shall make each of them a pair of shoes."

The husband consented willingly, and at night, when everything was finished, they laid the gifts together on the table, instead of the cut-out work, and placed themselves so that they could observe how the little men would behave. When midnight came, they rushed in, ready to set to work, but when they found, instead of the pieces of prepared leather, the neat little garments put ready for them, they stood a moment in surprise, and then they testified the greatest delight. With the greatest swiftness they took up the pretty garments and slipped them on, singing,

"What spruce and dandy boys are we! No longer cobblers we will be."

Then they hopped and danced about, jumping over the chairs and tables, and at last they danced out at the door.

From that time they were never seen again; but it always went well with the shoemaker as long as he lived, and whatever he took in hand prospered.

SEMINAR PLAN

"The Elves and the Shoemaker" (1814)

Brothers Grimm

Ideas and Values: generosity, kindness, mystery, wealth.

Pre-Seminar

Content—Present relevant background information:

During the days prior to the seminar, have participants read the text in pairs at least once, taking turns reading aloud. On the day before the seminar, read the text aloud to the children, while four or more volunteers act out the text while you read.

Briefly summarize: The "Brothers Grimm" were actually Jacob (1785–1863) and Wilhelm (1786–1859) Grimm, two in a family of nine children, who were fascinated from an early age with the folk tales they heard in their native Germany. They spent most of their adult lives at several German universities, where they were librarians and professors of linguistics, folklore, and medieval studies. The first edition of the brothers' famous *Kinder und Hausmarchen* (*Children's and Household Tales*) was published in 1812–1814; it would see six full editions during their lifetimes, and they eventually recorded 200 numbered stories.

They are among the first collectors of folk tales in any country who succeeded in popularizing true folk material collected in the field.

State directly that our purpose in participating in this dialogue is to gain understanding of an especially powerful and ambiguous folk tale, and in particular, to discuss these ideas (among others): *generosity, kindness, mystery, wealth.*

Process—Prepare participants to participate in seminar discussion with a version of the following script:

> A Paideia Seminar is a collaborative, intellectual dialogue about a text, facilitated with open-ended questions.

The main purpose of seminar is to arrive at a fuller understanding of the textual ideas and values in "The Elves and the Shoemaker," of ourselves, and of each other.

As the facilitator, I am primarily responsible for asking challenging, open-ended questions, and I will take notes to keep up with the talk turns and flow of ideas. I will help move the discussion along in a productive direction by asking follow-up questions based on my notes.

As participants, I am asking you to think, listen, and speak candidly about your thoughts, reactions, and ideas. You can help each other do this by using each other's names.

You do not need to raise your hands in order to speak; rather, the discussion is collaborative in that you try to stay focused on the main speaker and wait your turn to talk.

You should try to both agree and disagree in a courteous, thoughtful manner. For example, you might say, "I disagree with Joanna because...," focusing on the ideas involved, not the individuals.

Now, let's think about how we normally participate in a discussion as a group. Is there a goal that we can set for ourselves that will help the flow and meaning of the seminar? For this seminar, I would suggest *TO FOCUS ON CHARACTERS IN THE STORY*.

Set group goal and display it for all to see.

Please consider the list of personal participation goals that I have listed on the board:

   to speak at least three times

   to refer to the text in detail

   to listen closely to others

   to ask questions of others

Is there one that is a particular challenge for you personally? Will you choose one goal from the list and commit to achieving it during the discussion we are about to have? Please write your personal goal at the top of your copy of the text.

Seminar

Opening—Identify main ideas from the text:

Name one word to describe the shoemaker and his wife at the beginning of the story? (round-robin response) Why did you choose that word? (spontaneous discussion)

Core—Focus/analyze textual details:

What's one word you would use to describe the elves? Why?

Why do you think the elves chose to help the shoemaker? Refer to the story.

Did the shoemaker and his wife deserve the help of the elves? Why or why not?

Now name one word to describe the shoemaker and his wife at the end of the story? How have they changed?

Why do you think the elves never came back to the shoemaker's house?

Closing—Personalize and apply the textual ideas:

What is the most significant lesson in this tale as it applies to your life?

Post-Seminar

Process—Assess individual and group participation in seminar discussion with an appropriate version of the following script:

Thank you for your focused and thoughtful participation in our seminar. As part of the post-seminar process, I would first like to ask you to take a few minutes to reflect on your relative success in meeting the personal process goal you set prior to beginning the discussion. Please review the goal you set for yourself and reflect in writing to what extent you met the goal. In addition, note why you think you performed as you did. (*Pause for reflection.*)

Would several volunteers please share your self-assessment and reflection?

Now I would like us to talk together about how we did in relation to the group process goal we set for ourselves (*TO FOCUS ON THE CHARACTERS IN THE STORY*). On a scale of one to ten, ten being perfect, how would you say we did? Why? (*Pause for discussion.*)

As always, our goal is continuous improvement, both as individual seminar participants and as citizens. Thanks again for your participation.

Content—Extend application of textual and discussion ideas:

Tell the children that together you will create a series of illustrated fairy and folk tales from many traditions. Have them work in groups of two or three to create illustrations of different parts of the story. Display the resulting art work in the classroom with a copy of the story. (Perhaps this will be the first in several seminars on classic fairy tales.)

SEMINAR PLAN

Washington Crossing the Delaware (1851)

Emanual Leutze (1815–1868)

SEMINAR PLAN

· · · · · · · · · · · · · · · · · ·

Washington Crossing the Delaware (1851)

Emanual Leutze (1815–1868)

Ideas and Values: America, heroism, leadership, myth

Pre-Seminar

Content—Present relevant background information:

In the week prior to the seminar, post the following terms on an Art Word Wall in the classroom (or add them to the class Word Wall if one already exists) and work with students to define them. Elements of Art: form, line, shape, color, texture, space, value. Principles of Art: emphasis, balance, harmony, variety, movement, rhythm, proportion, unity.

In addition, during the week prior to the seminar, display a color print of the painting for students to examine at their leisure.

On the day of the seminar, share the following background information about the artist and his time period:

- ◆ The German-born Emanual Leutze immigrated to the United States at a young age and was passionate about the ideals of the American republic. He typically painted large, dramatic portraits of meticulously researched historic events. The sheer size of this canvas, 12 by 21 feet, pulls anyone standing before it literally into the scene.

- ◆ This painting is set on Christmas night, 1776, when the leader of the Continental Army, George Washington, leads his dwindling band of soldiers across the treacherous Delaware River to attack the British force at Trenton, thereby reversing the series of defeats suffered during the summer and fall of that year.

- ◆ Upon its completion in 1851, Leutze displayed this painting in New York, hoping to attract a government commission for similar works. It was viewed by thousands of people, purchased by a private collector, and led to Leutze's commission to paint *Westward the Course of Empire Takes Its Way* in the U.S. Capitol.

Prior to the seminar, pass out copies of the print to a group of eleven volunteers and challenge them to reenact the scene in the painting via dramatic tableaux (with the students becoming the figures in the painting). Invite discussion of what they learned about the scene by reenacting it and what the rest of the participants learned from observing the reenactment.

Review the terms from the Elements and Principles of Art that are included in the Word Wall—focusing on those that might appear in your questions—and then…

State directly that our purpose in participating in this dialogue is to gain understanding of the ideas and values in the text. More specifically, our purpose is to discuss the following ideas, among others: *America, heroism, leadership, myth.*

Process—Prepare participants to participate in seminar discussion with a version of the following script:

A Paideia Seminar is a collaborative, intellectual dialogue about a text, facilitated with open-ended questions.

The main purpose of seminar is to arrive at a fuller understanding of the textual ideas and values in Leutze's painting, of ourselves, and of each other.

As the facilitator, I am primarily responsible for asking challenging, open-ended questions, and I will take notes to keep up with the talk turns and flow of ideas. I will help move the discussion along in a productive direction by asking follow-up questions based on my notes.

As participants, I am asking you to think, listen, and speak candidly about your thoughts, reactions, and ideas. You can help each other do this by using each other's names.

You do not need to raise your hands in order to speak; rather, the discussion is collaborative in that you try to stay focused on the speaker and wait your turn to talk.

You should try to agree or disagree in a courteous, thoughtful manner. For example, you might say, "I disagree with…because…," focusing on the ideas involved, not the individuals.

Now, let's think about how we normally participate in a discussion as a group. Is there a goal that we can set for ourselves that will help the flow and meaning of the seminar? For this seminar, I would suggest *TO REFER TO THE TEXT IN DETAIL*.

Set group goal and display it for all to see.

Please consider the list of personal participation goals that I have listed on the board:

to speak at least three times

to refer to the text in detail

to keep an open mind

to speak out of uncertainty

Is there one that is a particular challenge for you personally? Will you choose one goal from the list and commit to achieving it during the discussion we are about to have? Please write your personal goal at the top of your copy of the text.

Have students work in pairs to sketch the contents of the painting. Let them know that they can add notes to their sketches (on color, texture, etc.) during the course of the discussion.

Seminar

Opening—Identify main ideas from the text:

What one word title would you give this painting? (round-robin response) Why? (spontaneous discussion)

Core— Focus/analyze textual details:

What do you think is the most important detail in this painting? Why?

Where is the light coming from in this painting? How can you tell?

Pick a figure in the painting other than Washington. What emotion do you think the figure in the painting is feeling? What in the painting makes you think this?

Tell students that they can now add to their original sketches based on the discussion thus far. Allow several minutes for participants to work.

What details did you choose to add to your sketch? Why?

Is there any sense of movement suggested by the painting? What effect does this sense of movement (or lack of movement) have?

What do you think this painting is saying about leadership? Refer to the painting in detail.

Closing—Personalize and apply the textual ideas:

Which figure in this painting do you most identify with? Why?

Post-Seminar

Process—Assess individual and group participation in seminar discussion with an appropriate version of the following script:

Thank you for your focused and thoughtful participation in our seminar. As part of the post-seminar process, I would first like to ask you to take a few minutes to reflect on your relative success in meeting the personal process goal you set prior to beginning the discussion. Please review the goal you set for yourself and reflect in writing to what extent you met the goal. In addition, note why you think you performed as you did. (*Pause for reflection.*)

Would several volunteers please share your self-assessment and reflection?

Now I would like us to talk together about how we did in relation to the group process goal we set for ourselves (*TO REFER TO THE TEXT IN DETAIL*). On a scale of one to ten, ten being perfect, how would you say we did? Why? (*Pause for discussion.*)

As always, our goal is continuous improvement, both as individual seminar participants and as citizens. Thanks again for your participation.

Content—Extend application of textual and discussion ideas:

Let students work in groups of two or three to choose from a list of historical events. Have them work together to sketch a version of the event that could be painted as a mural in your school. Then, have the groups make the case in writing for creating the mural.

SEMINAR PLAN

. . . .

"Axioms, or Laws of Motion"

from *Mathematical Principles of Natural Philosophy*

by Sir Isaac Newton

LAW I Every body continues in its state of rest, or of uniform motion in a right line, unless it is compelled to change that state by forces impressed upon it. PROJECTILES continue in their motions, so far as they are not retarded by the resistance of the air, or impelled downwards by the force of gravity. A top, whose parts by their cohesion are continually drawn aside from rectilinear motions, does not cease its rotation, otherwise than as it is retarded by the air. The greater bodies of the planets and comets, meeting with less resistance in freer spaces, preserve their motions both progressive and circular for a much longer time.

LAW II The change of motion is proportional to the motive force impressed; and is made in the direction of the right line in which that force is impressed. If any force generates motion, a double force will generate double the motion, a triple force triple the motion, whether that force be impressed altogether and at once, or gradually and successively. And this motion (being always directed the same way with the generating force), if the body moved before, is added to or subtracted from the former motion, according as they directly conspire with or are directly contrary to each other; or obliquely joined, when they are oblique, so as to produce a new motion compounded from the determination of both.

LAW III To every action there is always opposed an equal reaction: or, the mutual actions of two bodies upon each other are always equal, and directed to contrary parts. Whatever draws or presses another is as much drawn or pressed by that other. If you press a stone with your finger, the finger is also pressed by the stone. If a horse draws a stone tied to a rope, the horse (if I may say so) will be equally drawn back towards the stone; for the distended rope, by the same endeavour to relax or unbend itself, will draw the horse as much as it does the stone towards the horse, and will obstruct the progress of the one as much as it advances that of the other. For, because the motions are equally changed, the changes of the velocities made towards contrary parts are inversely proportional to the bodies. This law takes place also in attractions, as will be proved in the next Scholium....

SEMINAR PLAN

. . . .

"Axioms, or Laws of Motion"

Sir Isaac Newton (1642–1727)

from *Mathematical Principles of Natural Philosophy* (1687)

Ideas and Values: law, motion, order, physics

Pre-Seminar

Content—Present relevant background information:

Sir Isaac Newton is among the handful of history's most famous scientists. In addition to his highly original and influential work in optics and physics, he was also a highly creative and important mathematician and played a significant role in university as well as national politics. His *Mathematical Principles of Natural Philosophy* defines what has come to be known as Newtonian Physics, and although many of his ideas have been revised by the work of twentieth-century physicists, his Laws of Motion remain fundamental to an understanding of the natural world.

♦ Ask all participants to skim the reading quickly (inspectional reading) and then number the sentences in each law.

♦ Divide participants into three groups. Assign each group a law to read and condense into two or three readable sentences (analytical reading).

♦ Ask each group to share their sentences with the whole class in order and teach their law to the rest with simple demonstrations and explanations.

♦ Have the entire group read the three laws again silently.

State directly that our purpose in participating in this dialogue is to gain understanding of the physical laws that govern motion. More specifically, our purpose is to discuss the following ideas, among others: *law, motion, order, physics*.

Process—Prepare participants to participate in seminar discussion with a version of the following script:

> A Paideia Seminar is a collaborative, intellectual dialogue about a text, facilitated with open-ended questions.
>
> The main purpose of seminar is to arrive at a fuller understanding of the textual ideas and values, of ourselves, and of each other.
>
> I am primarily responsible for asking challenging, open-ended questions, and I will take notes to keep up with the talk turns and flow of ideas. I will help move the discussion along in a productive direction by asking follow-up questions based on my notes.
>
> I am asking you to think, listen, and speak candidly about your thoughts, reactions, and ideas. You can help each other do this by using each other's names.
>
> You do not need to raise your hands in order to speak; rather, the discussion is collaborative in that you try to stay focused on the main speaker and wait your turn to talk.
>
> You should try to both agree and disagree in a courteous, thoughtful manner. For example, you might say, "I disagree with Joanna because…," focusing on the ideas involved, not the individuals.
>
> Now, let's think about how we normally participate in a discussion as a group. Is there a goal that we can set for ourselves that will help the flow and meaning of the seminar? For this text, I would recommend: *TO ASK OUR GENUINE QUESTIONS.*

Set group goal and display it for all to see.

> Please consider the list of personal participation goals that I have listed on the board:
>
> > to refer specifically to the text
> >
> > to ask for clarification
> >
> > to listen with a quiet mind
> >
> > to speak out of uncertainty

Is there one that is a particular challenge for you personally? Will you choose one goal from the list and commit to achieving it during the discussion we are about to have? Please write your personal goal at the top of your copy of the text.

Seminar

Opening—Identify main ideas from the text:

Which of the three laws is the most significant? (vote by show of hands) Why did you pick the law for which you voted? (spontaneous discussion)

Core—Focus/analyze textual details:

Newton's first Law implies that a ball at rest and a ball moving at a constant speed are similar. Why does he imply this? Do you agree?

In the second Law, Newton writes that "the change of motion is proportional to the motive force impressed." Based on the text, what did he mean by this statement?

The third Law contains one of the most famous statements in scientific literature: "To every action there is always opposed an equal reaction." Based on the text, what does this statement actually mean?

How are the three laws related?

Based on the text, do scientists think differently from non-scientists? If so, how?

Closing—Personalize and apply the textual ideas:

What did you learn about the physical world today, either from the text or from the discussion?

Post-Seminar

Process—Assess individual and group participation in seminar discussion with an appropriate version of the following script:

Thank you for your focused and thoughtful participation in our seminar.

As part of the post-seminar process, I would first like to ask you to take a few minutes to reflect on your relative success in meeting the personal process goal you set prior to beginning the discussion. Please review the goal you set for yourself and reflect in writing to what extent you met the goal. In addition, note why you think you performed as you did. (Pause for reflection.)

Would several volunteers please share your self-assessment and reflection?

Now I would like us to talk together about how we did in relation to the group process goal we set for ourselves (TO ASK OUR GENUINE QUESTIONS). On a scale of one to ten, ten being perfect, how would you say we did? Why? (Pause for discussion.)

As always, our goal is continuous improvement: both as individual seminar participants and as citizens. Thanks again for your participation.

Content—Extend application of textual and discussion ideas:

Explain to participants that they are involved in creating an edition of *The Illustrated Newton*, in which each of Newton's major points is illustrated by photographs as well as drawings or graphs. Divide the class into three groups and assign one Law to each group for students to illustrate. In each case, the group should assign one of Abbott's photographs to their Law and sketch an illustration to go with the photograph. Share the illustrations with the entire seminar group.

SEMINAR PLAN

Tell all the Truth but tell it slant

Tell all the Truth but tell it slant—
Success in Circuit lies
Too bright for our infirm Delight
The Truth's superb surprise
As Lightning to the Children eased
With explanation kind
The Truth must dazzle gradually
Or every man be blind—

—Emily Dickinson (c. 1868)

"Tell all the Truth but tell it slant" (c. 1868)

Emily Dickinson (1830–1886)

Ideas and Values: poetry, sight, tact, truth

Pre-Seminar

Content—Present relevant background information:

In the week prior to the seminar, have the participants read the poem several times, including at least once aloud.

Several days prior to the seminar, divide the participants into four groups and have each group carry out one of the following exercises and then share their findings with the entire group:

♦ Consider a copy of the poem that shows only the capitalized words (including the first word in each line); speculate about what a poem that emphasizes these particular words might mean and do.

♦ Consider a list of all the words in the poem in alphabetical order; speculate on what a poem made from these words might mean and do.

♦ Divide the poem into a series of four couplets; write a brief summary of each couplet. Share the summary.

♦ Using standard punctuation (comma, colon, semicolon, period), work together to punctuate the poem as a series of sentences in prose. What did you discover?

On the day of the seminar, share the following background information about the artist and her time period:

Emily Dickinson was one of the most important and influential American poets of the 19th century. Although Dickinson was a prolific private poet, fewer than a dozen of her nearly eighteen hundred poems were published during her lifetime. The work that was published during her lifetime was usually altered significantly by the publishers to fit the conventional poetic rules of the time. Dickinson's poems are unique for the era in which she wrote; they contain short lines, typically lack titles, and often use slant rhyme as well as unconventional capitalization and punctuation.

Although most of her acquaintances were probably aware of Dickinson's writing, it was not until after her death in 1886—when Lavinia, Emily's younger sister, discovered her cache of poems—that the breadth of Dickinson's work became apparent. A complete and mostly unaltered collection of her poetry became available for the first time in 1955 when *The Poems of Emily Dickinson* was published by scholar Thomas H. Johnson. Despite unfavorable reviews and skepticism of her literary prowess during the late nineteenth- and early twentieth-centuries, critics now consider Dickinson to be a major American poet.

State directly that our purpose in participating in this dialogue is to gain understanding of the ideas and values in the text. More specifically, our purpose is to discuss the following ideas, among others: *poetry, sight, tact, truth.*

Process—Prepare participants to participate in seminar discussion with a version of the following script:

A Paideia Seminar is a collaborative, intellectual dialogue about a text, facilitated with open-ended questions.

The main purpose of seminar is to arrive at a fuller understanding of the textual ideas and values in Dickinson's poem, of ourselves, and of each other.

As the facilitator, I am primarily responsible for asking challenging, open-ended questions, and I will take notes to keep up with the talk turns and flow of ideas. I will help move the discussion along in a productive direction by asking follow-up questions based on my notes.

As participants, I am asking you to think, listen, and speak candidly about your thoughts, reactions, and ideas. You can help each other do this by using each other's names.

You do not need to raise your hands in order to speak; rather, the discussion is collaborative in that you try to stay focused on the speaker and wait your turn to talk.

You should try to agree or disagree in a courteous, thoughtful manner. For example, you might say, "I disagree with…because…," focusing on the ideas involved, not the individuals.

Now, let's think about how we normally participate in a discussion as a group. Is there a goal that we can set for ourselves that will help the flow and meaning of the seminar? For this seminar, I would suggest *TO FOCUS ON THE IDEAS IN THE POEM*.

Set group goal and display it for all to see.

Please consider the list of personal participation goals that I have listed on the board:

> to speak at least three times
>
> to refer to the text in detail
>
> to keep an open mind
>
> to speak out of uncertainty

Is there one that is a particular challenge for you personally? Will you choose one goal from the list and commit to achieving it during the discussion we are about to have? Please write your personal goal at the top of your copy of the text.

Seminar

Opening—Identify main ideas from the text:

> Dickinson never gave her poems titles. If you were her editor, what one-word title would you give this poem? (round-robin response) Why? (spontaneous discussion)

Core—Focus/analyze textual details:

> Dickinson uses a number of words that might be synonyms for *truth*. Which of these do you think is most important? Why?

Unlike more traditional poets, Dickinson often capitalizes words for no grammatical reason. Pick one of the words (not the first word in a line), and ask yourself: Why do you think she chose to capitalize that word? Why do you think she capitalized those words (plural) as a group?

There are a number of references to sight or light (*bright, Lightning, dazzle, blind*) in the poem. Why do you think she chose these words in writing about truth?

Some scholars believe that this poem represents Dickinson's definition of poetry. If that is true, what do you think she is saying about poetry?

Closing—Personalize and apply the textual ideas:

Based on the poem and our conversation about it, how would you personally define the truth? How should it be "told"?

Post-Seminar

Process—Assess individual and group participation in seminar discussion with an appropriate version of the following script:

Thank you for your focused and thoughtful participation in our seminar. As part of the post-seminar process, I would first like to ask you to take a few minutes to reflect on your relative success in meeting the personal process goal you set prior to beginning the discussion. Please review the goal you set for yourself and reflect in writing to what extent you met the goal. In addition, note why you think you performed as you did. (*Pause for reflection.*)

Would several volunteers please share your self-assessment and reflection?

Now I would like us to talk together about how we did in relation to the group process goal we set for ourselves (*TO FOCUS ON THE IDEAS IN THE POEM*). On a scale of one to ten, ten being perfect, how would you say we did? Why? (*Pause for discussion.*)

As always, our goal is continuous improvement, both as individual seminar participants and as citizens. Thanks again for your participation.

Content—Extend application of textual and discussion ideas:

Have each student choose an important idea or value (perhaps from Mortimer Adler's list of 103 "Great Ideas") that he or she would like to write about. Using Dickinson's poem as a model, have them write a poem about that idea or value, naming it in the poem and stating their beliefs about it.

SEMINAR PLAN

....

from *The Meno* (c. 387 B.C.)

Plato (428/427 B.C.–348/347 B.C.)

Meno. Yes, Socrates; but what do you mean by saying that we do not learn, and that what we call learning is only a process of recollection? Can you teach me how this is?

Soc. I told you, Meno, just now that you were a rogue, and now you ask whether I can teach you, when I am saying that there is no teaching, but only recollection; and thus you imagine that you will involve me in a contradiction.

Meno. Indeed, Socrates, I protest that I had no such intention. I only asked the question from habit; but if you can prove to me that what you say is true, I wish that you would.

Soc. It will be no easy matter, but I will try to please you to the utmost of my power. Suppose that you call one of your numerous attendants, that I may demonstrate on him.

Meno. Certainly. Come hither, boy.

Soc. He is Greek, and speaks Greek, does he not?

Meno. Yes, indeed; he was born in the house.

Soc. Attend now to the questions which I ask him, and observe whether he learns of me or only remembers.

Meno. I will.

Soc. Tell me, boy, do you know that a figure like this is a square?

Boy. I do.

Soc. And you know that a square figure has these four lines equal?

Boy. Certainly.

Soc. And these lines which I have drawn through the middle of the square are also equal?

Boy. Yes.

Soc. A square may be of any size?

Boy. Certainly.

Soc. And if one side of the figure be of two feet, and the other side be of two feet, how much will the whole be? Let me explain: If in one direction the space was of two feet, and in other direction of one foot, the whole would be of two feet taken once?

Boy. Yes.

Soc. But since this side is also of two feet, there are twice two feet?

Boy. There are.

Soc. Then the square is of twice two feet?

Boy. Yes.

Soc. And how many are twice two feet? Count and tell me.

Boy. Four, Socrates.

Soc. And might there not be another square twice as large as this, and having like this the lines equal?

Boy. Yes.

Soc. And of how many feet will that be?

Boy. Of eight feet.

Soc. And now try and tell me the length of the line which forms the side of that double square: this is two feet—what will that be?

Boy. Clearly, Socrates, it will be double.

Soc. Do you observe, Meno, that I am not teaching the boy anything, but only asking him questions; and now he fancies that he knows how long a line is necessary in order to produce a figure of eight square feet; does he not?

Meno. Yes.

Soc. And does he really know?

Meno. Certainly not.

Soc. He only guesses that because the square is double, the line is double.

Meno. True.

Soc. Observe him while he recalls the steps in regular order. (to the Boy.) Tell me, boy, do you assert that a double space comes from a double line? Remember that I am not speaking of an oblong, but of a figure equal every way, and twice the size of this—that is to say of eight feet; and I want to know whether you still say that a double square comes from double line?

Boy. Yes.

Soc. But does not this line become doubled if we add another such line here?

Boy. Certainly.

Soc. And four such lines will make a space containing eight feet?

Boy. Yes.

Soc. Let us describe such a figure: Would you not say that this is the figure of eight feet?

Boy. Yes.

Soc. And are there not these four divisions in the figure, each of which is equal to the figure of four feet?

Boy. True.

Soc. And is not that four times four?

Boy. Certainly.

Soc. And four times is not double?

Boy. No, indeed.

Soc. But how much?

Boy. Four times as much.

Soc. Therefore the double line, boy, has given a space, not twice, but four times as much.

Boy. True.

Soc. Four times four are sixteen—are they not?

Boy. Yes.

Soc. What line would give you a space of right feet, as this gives one of sixteen feet—do you see?

Boy. Yes.

Soc. And the space of four feet is made from this half line?

Boy. Yes.

Soc. Good; and is not a space of eight feet twice the size of this, and half the size of the other?

Boy. Certainly.

Soc. Such a space, then, will be made out of a line greater than this one, and less than that one?

Boy. Yes; I think so.

Soc. Very good; I like to hear you say what you think. And now tell me, is not this a line of two feet and that of four?

Boy. Yes.

Soc. Then the line which forms the side of eight feet ought to be more than this line of two feet, and less than the other of four feet?

Boy. It ought.

Soc. Try and see if you can tell me how much it will be.

Boy. Three feet.

Soc. Then if we add a half to this line of two, that will be the line of three. Here are two and there is one; and on the other side, here are two also and there is one: and that makes the figure of which you speak?

Boy. Yes.

Soc. But if there are three feet this way and three feet that way, the whole space will be three times three feet?

Boy. That is evident.

Soc. And how much are three times three feet?

Boy. Nine.

Soc. And how much is the double of four?

Boy. Eight.

Soc. Then the figure of eight is not made out of three?

Boy. No.

Soc. But from what line?—tell me exactly; and if you would rather not reckon, try and show me the line.

Boy. Indeed, Socrates, I do not know.

Soc. Do you see, Meno, what advances he has made in his power of recollection? He did not know at first, and he does not know now, what is the side of a figure of eight feet: but then he thought that he knew, and answered confidently as if he knew, and had no difficulty; now he has a difficulty, and neither knows nor fancies that he knows.

Meno. True.

Soc. Is he not better off in knowing his ignorance?

Meno. I think that he is.

Soc. If we have made him doubt, and given him the "torpedo's shock," have we done him any harm?

Meno. I think not.

Soc. We have certainly, as would seem, assisted him in some degree to the discovery of the truth; and now he will wish to remedy his ignorance, but then he would have been ready to tell all the world again and again that the double space should have a double side.

Meno. True.

Soc. But do you suppose that he would ever have enquired into or learned what he fancied that he knew, though he was really ignorant of it, until he had fallen into perplexity under the idea that he did not know, and had desired to know?

Meno. I think not, Socrates.

Soc. Then he was the better for the torpedo's touch?

Meno. I think so.

Soc. Mark now the farther development. I shall only ask him, and not teach him, and he shall share the enquiry with me: and do you watch and see if you find me telling or explaining anything to him, instead of eliciting his opinion. Tell me, boy, is not this a square of four feet which I have drawn?

Boy. Yes.

Soc. And now I add another square equal to the former one?

Boy. Yes.

Soc. And a third, which is equal to either of them?

Boy. Yes.

Soc. Suppose that we fill up the vacant corner?

Boy. Very good.

Soc. Here, then, there are four equal spaces?

Boy. Yes.

Soc. And how many times larger is this space than this other?

Boy. Four times.

Soc. But it ought to have been twice only, as you will remember.

Boy. True.

Soc. And does not this line, reaching from corner to corner, bisect each of these spaces?

Boy. Yes.

Soc. And are there not here four equal lines which contain this space?

Boy. There are.

Soc. Look and see how much this space is.

Boy. I do not understand.

Soc. Has not each interior line cut off half of the four spaces?

Boy. Yes.

Soc. And how many spaces are there in this section?

Boy. Four.

Soc. And how many in this?

Boy. Two.

Soc. And four is how many times two?

Boy. Twice.

Soc. And this space is of how many feet?

Boy. Of eight feet.

Soc. And from what line do you get this figure?

Boy. From this.

Soc. That is, from the line which extends from corner to corner of the figure of four feet?

Boy. Yes.

Soc. And that is the line which the learned call the diagonal. And if this is the proper name, then you, Meno's slave, are prepared to affirm that the double space is the square of the diagonal?

Boy. Certainly, Socrates.

Soc. What do you say of him, Meno? Were not all these answers given out of his own head?

Meno. Yes, they were all his own.

Soc. And yet, as we were just now saying, he did not know?

Meno. True.

Soc. But still he had in him those notions of his—had he not?

Meno. Yes.

Soc. Then he who does not know may still have true notions of that which he does not know?

Meno. He has.

Soc. And at present these notions have just been stirred up in him, as in a dream; but if he were frequently asked the same questions, in different forms, he would know as well as any one at last?

Meno. I dare say.

Soc. Without any one teaching him he will recover his knowledge for himself, if he is only asked questions?

Meno. Yes.

Soc. And this spontaneous recovery of knowledge in him is recollection?

Meno. True.

Soc. And this knowledge which he now has must he not either have acquired or always possessed?

Meno. Yes.

Soc. But if he always possessed this knowledge he would always have known; or if he has acquired the knowledge he could not have acquired it in this life, unless he has been taught geometry; for he may be made to do the same with all geometry and every other branch of knowledge. Now, has any one ever taught him all this? You must know about him, if, as you say, he was born and bred in your house.

Meno. And I am certain that no one ever did teach him.

Soc. And yet he has the knowledge?

Meno. The fact, Socrates, is undeniable.

Soc. But if he did not acquire the knowledge in this life, then he must have had and learned it at some other time?

Meno. Clearly he must.

Soc. Which must have been the time when he was not a man?

Meno. Yes.

Soc. And if there have been always true thoughts in him, both at the time when he was and was not a man, which only need to be awakened into knowledge by putting questions to him, his soul must have always possessed this knowledge, for he always either was or was not a man?

Meno. Obviously.

Soc. And if the truth of all things always existed in the soul, then the soul is immortal. Wherefore be of good cheer, and try to recollect what you do not know, or rather what you do not remember.

Meno. I feel, somehow, that I like what you are saying.

Soc. And I, Meno, like what I am saying. Some things I have said of which I am not altogether confident. But that we shall be better and braver and less helpless if we think that we ought to enquire, than we should have been if we indulged in the idle fancy that there was no knowing and no use in seeking to know what we do not know;—that is a theme upon which I am ready to fight, in word and deed, to the utmost of my power.

SEMINAR PLAN

· · · · · · · · · · · · · · · · · · ·

from *The Meno* (c. 387 B.C.)

Plato (428/427 B.C.–348/347 B.C.)

Ideas and Values: learning, questioning, thinking, truth, wisdom

Pre-Seminar

Content—Present relevant background information:

Have participants read the text three times (inspectional, analytical, syntopical).

♦ First, ask them to read the entire text quickly for homework, using three different highlighters to highlight the names of Socrates, Meno, and the Slave Boy, so that they can see at a glance the structure of the dialogue. During this first reading, they should also mark unfamiliar vocabulary and add to their personal dictionaries (in their journals).

♦ Second, have them read the dialogue aloud in groups of three. Two days prior to the seminar, assign reading groups of three each; have them choose roles and read the entire dialogue aloud. As time permits, have them discuss the roles of the three characters in the dialogue.

♦ Third, have them read the dialogue silently in class the day before the seminar using the attached graphic organizer that asks for text to self, text to text, and text to other text connections. During this reading, list the earlier seminar texts in the "wisdom" unit on the board as possibilities for "text to other text" connections.

On the day of the seminar, display the diagram of the "square within the square" on the board for participants to refer to during the discussion.

Prior to the seminar, share the following background information:

Plato was a Classical Greek philosopher, mathematician, writer of philosophical dialogues, and founder of the Academy in Athens, the first institution of higher learning in the Western world. Along with his mentor, Socrates, and his student, Aristotle, Plato helped to lay the foundations of natural philosophy, science, and Western philosophy. Plato was originally a student of Socrates, and was much influenced by his thinking.

State directly that our purpose in participating in this dialogue is to gain understanding of the ideas and values in the text. More specifically, our purpose is to discuss the following ideas, among others: *learning, questioning, thinking, truth, wisdom.*

Process—Prepare participants to participate in seminar discussion with a version of the following script:

A Paideia Seminar is a thoughtful discussion where we work with others to understand important ideas.

The main purpose for discussing this excerpt from *The Meno* is to better understand learning, questioning, thinking, truth, and wisdom—to better understand what we think of these ideas as well as how others view them.

During this discussion, we're going to practice focusing on the details in the text.

You do not need to raise your hands in order to speak; try to stay focused on the main speaker and wait your turn to talk.

We'll also practice listening by using others' names and paraphrasing what we hear others saying. We will agree and disagree in a courteous, thoughtful manner.

As the facilitator, my job is to ask challenging, open-ended questions. I will take some notes to help me keep up with the talk turns and flow of ideas.

Now, let's do a little self-assessment. Based on our other discussions, I'm going to suggest that out group goal be *TO USE LANGUAGE AS PRECISELY AS POSSIBLE.*

Display group goal for all to see.

Now think about how you usually participate in our seminars. What would be a good goal for you today? Maybe you'd like to choose from one of these:

to make specific references to the text

to make connections between ideas

to identify contradictions

to keep an open mind

Please write your personal goal at the top of your copy of the text.

Seminar

Opening—Identify main ideas from the text:

Our text is an excerpt from a longer work by Plato. What do you think would be a good title for this excerpt? (round-robin response) Why? (spontaneous discussion)

Core—Focus/analyze textual details:

What is one word you would use to describe Socrates as he is portrayed here? What in the text makes you think this?

Why do you think Plato chooses a math problem to illustrate Socrates' belief that "learning is recollection"?

Why do you think he chooses a "slave boy" as Socrates' student?

At one point, Socrates turns to Meno and says of the Boy that "now he fancies that he knows how long a line is necessary in order to produce a figure of eight square feet; does he not?" Meno replies that he does but that he is mistaken. What does this passage suggest about learning math? About any subject?

How would you respond to Socrates' question: "Were not all these answers given out of his own head?" Do you agree with him?

Based on the text, what would Socrates say *thinking* is?

Closing— Personalize and apply the textual ideas:

What have you learned from this text—and our discussion?

Post-Seminar

Process—Assess individual and group participation in seminar discussion:

> Thank you for your focused and thoughtful participation in our seminar.
>
> Take a few minutes to reflect on your relative success in meeting the personal process goal you set prior to the discussion. Please review the goal you set for yourself and briefly describe in writing to what extent you met the goal. In addition, please note why you performed as you did.
>
> (*Pause for reflection*).
>
> How did we do as a group? Let's rate our seminar from 0 to 5, with 5 meaning perfect and 0 meaning we really need improvement. With a hand signal, how would you rate our seminar for today?
>
> Now, would someone say why you gave us the rating you did?
>
> Our group goal was to USE LANGUAGE AS PRECISELY AS POSSIBLE. How did we do with that goal in particular?
>
> (*Pause for discussion.*)
>
> Now, would someone volunteer to share your self-assessment and reflection?
>
> (*Invite students to share how they did as individuals and help them identify an appropriate goal for the next seminar.*)
>
> What should we work on together next seminar? As always, our goal is continuous improvement, both as individual seminar participants and as citizens. Thanks again for your participation.

Content—Extend application of textual and discussion ideas:

Have students respond to the following prompt by writing for no more than one hour. Prompt: Write a personal definition in several paragraphs of one of the following terms: *learning, questioning, thinking, truth, wisdom.* Please refer in detail to our excerpt from *The Meno.* You may use your copy of the text along with your notes. Your definition will be graded on its clarity, coherence, and flexibility.

SEMINAR PLAN

from *On Liberty*

Chapter Two: "On the Liberty of Thought and Discussion"

by John Stuart Mill

It still remains to speak of one of the principal causes which make diversity of opinion advantageous, and will continue to do so until mankind shall have entered a stage of intellectual advancement which at present seems at an incalculable distance. We have hitherto considered only two possibilities: that the received opinion may be false, and some other opinion, consequently, true; or that, the received opinion being true, a conflict with the opposite error is essential to a clear apprehension and deep feeling of its truth. But there is a commoner case than either of these; when the conflicting doctrines, instead of being one true and the other false, share the truth between them; and the nonconforming opinion is needed to supply the remainder of the truth, of which the received doctrine embodies only a part. Popular opinions, on subjects not palpable to sense, are often true, but seldom or never the whole truth. They are a part of the truth; sometimes a greater, sometimes a smaller part, but exaggerated, distorted, and disjointed from the truths by which they ought to be accompanied and limited. Heretical opinions, on the other hand, are generally some of these suppressed and neglected truths, bursting the bonds which kept them down, and either seeking reconciliation with the truth contained in the common opinion, or fronting it as enemies, and setting themselves up, with similar exclusiveness, as the whole truth. The latter case is hitherto the most frequent, as, in the human mind, one-sidedness has always been the rule, and many-sidedness the exception. Hence, even in revolutions of opinion, one part of the truth usually sets while another rises. Even progress, which ought to superadd, for the most part only substitutes, one partial and incomplete truth for another; improvement consisting chiefly in this, that the new fragment of truth is more wanted, more adapted to the needs of the time, than that which it displaces. Such being the partial character of prevailing opinions, even when resting on a true foundation, every opinion which embodies somewhat of the portion of truth which the common opinion omits, ought to be considered precious, with whatever amount of error and confusion that truth may be blended. No sober judge of human affairs will feel bound to be indignant because those who force on our notice truths which we should otherwise have overlooked, overlook some of those which we see. Rather, he will think that so long as popular truth is one-sided, it is more desirable than otherwise that unpopular truth should have one-sided assertors too; such being usually the most energetic, and the most likely to compel reluctant attention to the fragment of wisdom which they proclaim as if it were the whole.

SEMINAR PLAN

. . . .

from *On Liberty* (1859)

John Stuart Mill (1806–1873)

Ideas and Values: dialogue, free thought, truth, authority

Pre-Seminar

Content—Present relevant background information:

Ask participants to take part in the following "Opinion Corners" activity:

1. Post signs in the four corners of the classroom: *Strongly Agree, Agree, Disagree, Strongly Disagree.*

2. Write on the board the following quote from the text: "Popular opinions are often true, but seldom or never the whole truth."

3. Have participants move to the corner that reflects their response to this statement.

4. Give participants three to five minutes to discuss in their corners why they chose that response. Have each group select a spokesperson to share their ideas.

5. Each spokesperson in turn summarizes that group's thinking.

6. (*optional depending on time*) Have participants spend about five minutes expressing the counter argument in writing.

Share appropriate points from the following background information:

♦ John Stewart Mill was a social philosopher.

♦ He married his long-time friend, Mrs. Harriet Taylor, and with her was an advocate of women's rights.

♦ He wrote on politics and philosophy, including the very influential *On Liberty* (1859), addressing the nature and limits of power that can be legitimately exercised by society over the individual.

♦ John Stuart Mill was born in London and taught by his father—a philosopher from Scotland; his education was massive in scope and equipped Mill by the time he was thirteen with the equivalent of a thorough university education.

♦ Although Mill never actually broke off relations with his father (and his father's intellectual circle), he suffered an emotional and intellectual crisis when he was 20, leading to his eventually questioning all the received knowledge of his age.

Number the sentences of the text 1 to 12.

Read the excerpt from *On Liberty* at least once.

State directly that our purpose in participating in this dialogue is to gain understanding of the roles individual human beings play in a democratic society. More specifically, our purpose is to discuss the following ideas, among others: *dialogue, free thought, truth, authority.*

Process—Prepare participants to participate in seminar discussion with a version of the following script:

A Paideia Seminar is a collaborative, intellectual dialogue about a text, facilitated with open-ended questions.

The main purpose of seminar is to arrive at a fuller understanding of the textual ideas and values, of ourselves, and of each other.

I am primarily responsible for asking challenging, open-ended questions, and I will take notes to keep up with the talk turns and flow of ideas. I will help move the discussion along in a productive direction by asking follow-up questions based on my notes.

I am asking you to think, listen, and speak candidly about your thoughts, reactions, and ideas. You can help each other do this by using each other's names.

You do not need to raise your hands in order to speak; rather, the discussion is collaborative in that you try to stay focused on the main speaker and wait your turn to talk.

You should try to both agree and disagree in a courteous, thoughtful manner. For example, you might say, "I disagree with Joanna because…," focusing on the ideas involved, not the individuals.

Now, let's think about how we normally participate in a discussion as a group. Is there a goal that we can set for ourselves that will help the flow and meaning of the seminar? For this seminar, I would suggest *TO BUILD ON OTHERS' COMMENTS*.

Set group goal and display it for all to see.

Please consider the list of personal participation goals that I have listed on the board.

to speak at least three times

to refer to the text

to ask a question

to speak out of uncertainty

Is there one that is a particular challenge for you personally? Will you choose one goal from the list and commit to achieving it during the discussion we are about to have? Please write your personal goal at the top of your copy of the text.

Seminar

Opening—Identify main ideas from the text:

With participants new to seminar: What sentence or part of a sentence could serve as a title for this paragraph? (round robin, give paragraph and sentence number)

With participants experienced with seminar: What sentence or part of a sentence do you find most challenging? (hopping robin, give paragraph and sentence number)

Why did you choose that passage? (spontaneous discussion)

Core—Focus/analyze textual details:

Mill argues in this paragraph that the most common case is "when the conflicting doctrines, instead of being one true and the other false, share the truth between them; and the nonconforming opinion is needed to supply the remainder of the truth, of which the received doctrine embodies only a part." Mill uses the phrases "one-sided" and "many-sided" to describe an individual's potential perspectives in response to an issue. What do you think he means by these phrases?

Which is more important to the intellectual life of a seminar: the one-sided perspective or the many-sided perspective? Why?

Mill implies throughout this paragraph that in order to attain "intellectual advancement," we must search for the truth. In what ways is a Paideia Seminar a search for the truth?

Closing—Personalize and apply the textual ideas:

What do Mill's arguments about the search for the truth have to do with life in a democracy? What do they teach us about our role as citizens in a democracy?

Post-Seminar

Process—Assess individual and group participation in seminar discussion with an appropriate version of the following script:

Thank you for your focused and thoughtful participation in our seminar.

As part of the post-seminar process, I would first like to ask you to take a few minutes to reflect on your relative success in meeting the personal process goal you set prior to beginning the discussion. Please review the goal you set for yourself and reflect in writing to what extent you met the goal. In addition, note why you think you performed as you did. (*Pause for reflection.*)

Would several volunteers please share your self-assessment and reflection?

Now I would like us to talk together about how we did in relation to the group process goal we set for ourselves (*TO BUILD ON OTHERS' COMMENTS*). On a scale of one to ten, ten being perfect, how would you say we did? Why? (*Pause for discussion.*)

As always, our goal is continuous improvement, both as individual seminar participants and as citizens. Thanks again for your participation.

Content—Extend application of textual and discussion ideas:

Ask participants to write for four to five minutes about an important social issue—one that they tend to be "one-sided" about.

Then ask them to add to their statement the arguments from other perspectives (perhaps heard during the seminar) to create a view of the issue that is "many-sided."

Finally, ask that they write a concluding paragraph in which they merge one or more perspectives into a comprehensive statement.

Bibliography

Adler, Mortimer J. (1982). *The Paideia Proposal*. New York: Macmillan.

Adler, Mortimer J. (1983). *How to Speak How to Listen*. New York: Macmillan.

Adler, Mortimer J. (1990). *Reforming Education: The Opening of the American Mind*. New York: Collier.

Adler, Mortimer J., & Charles van Doren. (1972). *How to Read a Book*. New York: Simon & Schuster.

Augustine, Saint. (413–426/1952). *The City of God*. Vol. 18 Great Books of the Western World. Chicago: Encyclopedia Britannica.

Anderson, Lorin, & David Krathwohl. (2001). *A Taxonomy for Learning, Teaching, and Assessing*. New York: Longman.

Aristotle (~366 B.C./1952). *Rhetoric*. Vol. 9 Great Books of the Western World. Chicago: Encyclopedia Britannica.

Bacon, Francis. (1601/1942). "Of Custom and Education" in *Essays and New Atlantis*. Roslyn, NY: Walter J. Black, pp. 165–67.

Bacon, Francis. (1601/1942). "Of Studies" in *Essays and New Atlantis*. Roslyn, NY: Walter J. Black, pp. 207–09.

Bacon, Francis. (1623/1952). *Advancement of Learning*. Vol. 30 Great Books of the Western World. Chicago: Encyclopedia Britannica.

Barker, Larry, & Kittie Watson. (2000). *Listen Up: How to Improve Relationships, Reduce Stress, and Be More Productive by Using the Power of Listening*. New York: St. Martin's.

Barzun, Jacques. (1959). *The House of Intellect*. New York: Harper & Brothers.

Billings, Laura, & Jill Fitzgerald. (2003). "Dialogic Discussion and the Paideia Seminar." *American Educational Research Journal*. Vol. 39, No. 4, 907–41.

Cicero. (44 B.C./1991). *On Duties*. Cambridge: Cambridge University Press.

Claxton, Guy. (1997). *Hare Brain, Tortoise Mind: Why Intelligence Increases When You Think Less*. New York: Ecco Press.

Deason, Terrence W. (1997). *The Symbolic Species: The Co-Evolution of Language and the Brain*. New York: W.W. Norton.

Derrida, Jacques. (1967/1997). *Of Grammatology*. Translated by Gayatri Chakravorty Spivak. Baltimore, MD: Johns Hopkins.

Friedman, Thomas L. (2005). *The World Is Flat: A Brief History of the Twenty-First Century*. New York: Farrar, Straus and Giroux.

Gardner, Howard. (1993). *Creating Minds: An Anatomy of Creativity Seen Through the Lives of Freud, Einstein, Picasso, Stravinsky, Eliot, Graham, and Gandhi*. New York: Basic Books.

Gardner, Howard. (1999). *Intelligence Reframed: Multiple Intelligences for the 21st Century*. New York: Basic Books.

Grudin, Robert. (1996). *On Dialogue: An Essay in Free Thought*. Boston: Houghton Mifflin.

Harvey, Stephanie, & Anne Goudvis. (2000). *Strategies That Work: Teaching Comprehension to Enhance Understanding*. Portland, ME: Stenhouse.

Hobbes, Thomas. (1651/1952). *Leviathan; Or, Matter, Form, and Power of a Commonwealth Ecclesiastical and Civil*. Vol. 23. Great Books of the Western World. Chicago: Encyclopedia Britannica.

Hurson, Tim. (2008). *Think Better: An Innovator's Guide to Productive Thinking*. New York: McGraw Hill.

Hutchins, Robert M. (1952). *The Great Conversation: The Substance of a Liberal Education*. Introduction to the Great Books of the Western World. Chicago: Encyclopedia Britannica.

Keats, John (2009). *Selected Letters*. Robert Gittings, ed. New York: Oxford University Press.

Locke, John. (1690/1952). *Essay Concerning Human Understanding*. Vol. 35. Great Books of the Western World. Chicago: Encyclopedia Britannica.

Marzano, Robert J., & John S. Kendall. (2008). *Designing and Assessing Educational Objectives: Applying the New Taxonomy*. Thousand Oaks, CA: Corwin.

Mill, John Stuart. (1859/1952). *On Liberty*. Vol. 43 Great Books of the Western World. Chicago: Encyclopedia Britannica.

Montaigne, Michel Eyquem de. (1577/1952). "The Art of Conference." Vol. 25 Great Books of the Western World. Chicago: Encyclopedia Britannica.

Nichols, Maria. (2006). *Comprehension Through Conversation*. Portsmouth, NH: Heinemann.

Nichols, Maria. (2008). *Talking About Text: Guiding Students to Increase Comprehension Through Purposeful Talk*. Shell Education.

Nichols, Michael P. (1995). *The Lost Art of Listening: How Learning to Listen Can Improve Relationships*. New York: Guilford.

Noddings, Nel. (2008). "All Our Students Thinking" in *Educational Leadership*, 65 (5), pp. 8–13.

Paul, Richard, & Linda Elder. (2001). *Critical Thinking: Tools for Taking Charge of Your Learning and Your Life*. Upper Saddle River, NJ: Prentice Hall.

Phillips, Vicki and Carina Wong. (2010). "Tying Together the Common Core Standards, Instruction, and Assessments." In *Kappan*, 91 (5), pp. 37–42.

Pihlgren, Ann S. (2008). *Socrates in the Classroom: Rationales and Effects of Philosophizing with Children*. Stockholm University: Department of Education.

Pink, Daniel H. (2005). *A Whole New Mind: Moving from the Information Age to the Conceptual Age*. New York: Penguin.

Plato. (c. 387 b.c. /1952). *The Meno*. Translated by Benjamin Jowett. Vol. 7 Great Books of the Western World. Chicago: Encyclopedia Britannica.

Roberts, Terry, & Laura Billings. (1999). *The Paideia Classroom: Teaching for Understanding*. Larchmont, NY: Eye On Education.

Roberts, Terry, & Laura Billings. (2008). "Thinking Is Literacy, Literacy Thinking." *Educational Leadership*. Vol. 65, No. 5, 32–36.

Schultz, Katherine. (2009). *Rethinking Classroom Participation: Listening to Silent Voices*. New York: Teachers College Press.

Stiggins, Rick, Judith A. Arter, Jan Chappuis, & Stephen Chappuis. (2007). *Classroom Assessment for Student Learning: Doing It Right—Using It Well*. Merrill Education.

Strunk, William, Jr., & E. B White. (1979). *The Elements of Style*. Third Edition. New York: MacMillan.

Tovani, Chris. (2000). *I Read It, but I Don't Get It: Comprehension Strategies for Adolescent Readers*. Portland, ME: Stenhouse.

Vygotsky, Lev. (1934/1986). *Thought and Language*. Cambridge, MA: MIT Press.

Wiggins, Grant. (1999). *Assessing Student Performance: Exploring the Purpose and Limits of Testing*. San Francisco: Jossey Bass.

Wiggins, Grant, & Jay McTighe. (2001). *Understanding by Design*. Alexandria, VA: ASCD.

Zinsser, William. (1988). *Writing to Learn*. New York: Harper & Row.

Glossary

Cognitive dissonance: Psychologists tell us that when we are forced to deal with contradictory points of view, especially about a topic that is important to us, we suffer from *cognitive dissonance*, the result of mental disequilibrium (see below). In this state, our minds will often reject any information that contradicts our own beliefs, causing us to consciously or subconsciously dismiss what we are hearing. Therefore, it requires a deliberately open mind to overcome cognitive dissonance and think successfully about sophisticated topics.

Fluency: Mastery in the flow of language, typically thought of as fluency in speech or even writing. Here, we also mean fluency in interpreting the written and spoken words of others.

Maieutic and Socratic questions: *Maieutic* derives from the Greek word for midwifery and so refers to those truly open-ended questions that are genuinely intended to elicit (i.e., help in the birth of) the ideas of others. *Socratic*, on the other hand, is typically used to describe more leading questions intended to elicit a pre-determined response. Experienced facilitators of Paideia Seminars use both types of questions—deliberately—to facilitate discussion.

Mental equilibrium and disequilibrium: Cognitive equilibrium means a confidence and assurance that one's attitude or perspective is valid. During a seminar discussion, one's sense of certainty is often disturbed by other points of view, and disequilibrium results. The world becomes more complex and demanding, so we are forced to work harder to explain and manipulate it successfully. In most instances, however, a new, more sophisticated, more inclusive explanation emerges, and mental equilibrium is re-established. A heightened state of understanding is the result.

Negative capability: simply put, comfort with uncertainty. Following Keats' famous definition, "Men [and Women] of Achievement" are capable of speaking comfortably out of uncertainty, mystery, and doubt. Negative capability is more than listening with an open mind; it involves speaking with a proactive desire to combine elements in new and creative relationships.

Paideia Seminar: a collaborative intellectual dialogue facilitated with open-ended questions about a text. It nurtures basic speaking and listening as well as reading and writing skills—the literacy skills that make up thinking.

Text: a set of interrelated ideas, often represented in a human artifact. Texts can include books, problems, experiments, and other artifacts; they are not limited to works in the form of printed language.

Thinking: the ability to explain and manipulate a text. By *text*, we mean a set of interrelated ideas, often represented in a human artifact. Learning to think, then, is the process of explaining and manipulating increasingly complex texts successfully. By definition, increasingly complex texts contain larger numbers of discrete elements and more complex relationships between and among those elements.

Understanding: the ability to explain and manipulate the material under consideration. True understanding is deeper and more sophisticated than simple memorization; it is the result of successful analysis and synthesis. It is the goal of seminar discussion.